HORUS BOOKS

SUPER STRUCTURES

Philip Brooks

HORUS EDITIONS

Published by Horus Editions
Award Publications Limited,
1st Floor, 27 Longford Street,
London NW1 3DZ

Copyright © 2000 Horus Editions

Series editor Elizabeth Miles
Designed by Steve Weston, Richard Rowan, Paul Richards
Illustrations by Sebastian Quigley, Steve Weston,
Julian Baker Illustrations, Terry Hadler, Ian Howatson,
Martin Sanders and Steve Seymour

ISBN 1-899762-48-5 (Cased)
ISBN 1-899762-50-7 (Paperback)

Printed in Singapore

HOW IT WORKS

CONTENTS

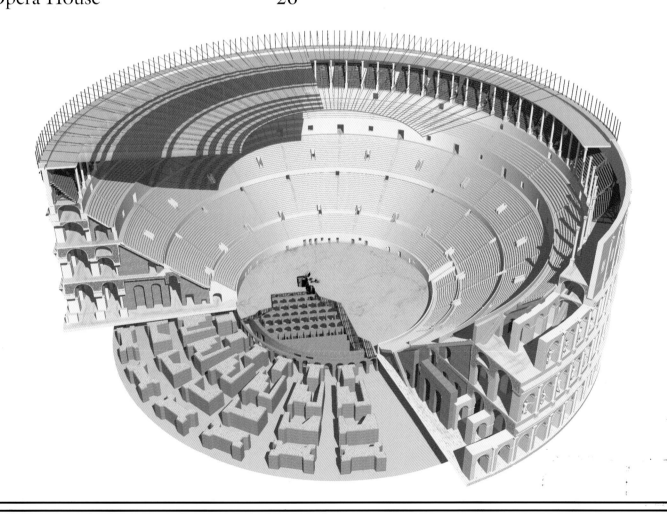

Pyramids

THE ANCIENT pyramids of Egypt were built more than 4500 years ago. They were huge tombs in which the pharaohs (rulers) of Egypt were buried with treasures that they thought were needed in the after-life. Around 2.3 million limestone blocks, each weighing 2500 kilograms or more, were used to build the Great Pyramid of Pharaoh Khufu (*right*). The builders had no wheels or complex machines, so the stones were hauled on sledges along a path of logs. The pyramid-builders began by making the site level and marking out the area of the base. Then they dug out the underground tomb and passageways. Next, the pyramid was built up in stepped layers. Finally, the sides of the pyramid were covered with polished white limestone blocks to make them smooth and shiny.

GRANITE BLOCKS WERE DESIGNED TO STOP THE BURIAL CHAMBER FROM COLLAPSING UNDER THE WEIGHT OF THE STONE ABOVE

THE PHARAOH'S MUMMIFIED BODY WAS PLACED IN THIS DECORATED CHAMBER, ALONG WITH HIS BELONGINGS

Raising the stones

No one knows for sure how the huge blocks of stone were raised to build the pyramid. Many people think that the builders made ramps out of earth and rubble, which spiralled around the half-finished pyramid. Others think that levers were used to raise each block slightly, so that material could be pushed underneath. Gradually in this way, the stone could be raised to the next level. A vast army of workers was needed and the building took some 20 years.

BEFORE BURIAL, THE KING'S BODY WAS PREPARED IN THE MORTUARY TEMPLE

A STONE CAUSEWAY WAS BUILT FROM THE RIVER NILE TO THE PYRAMID

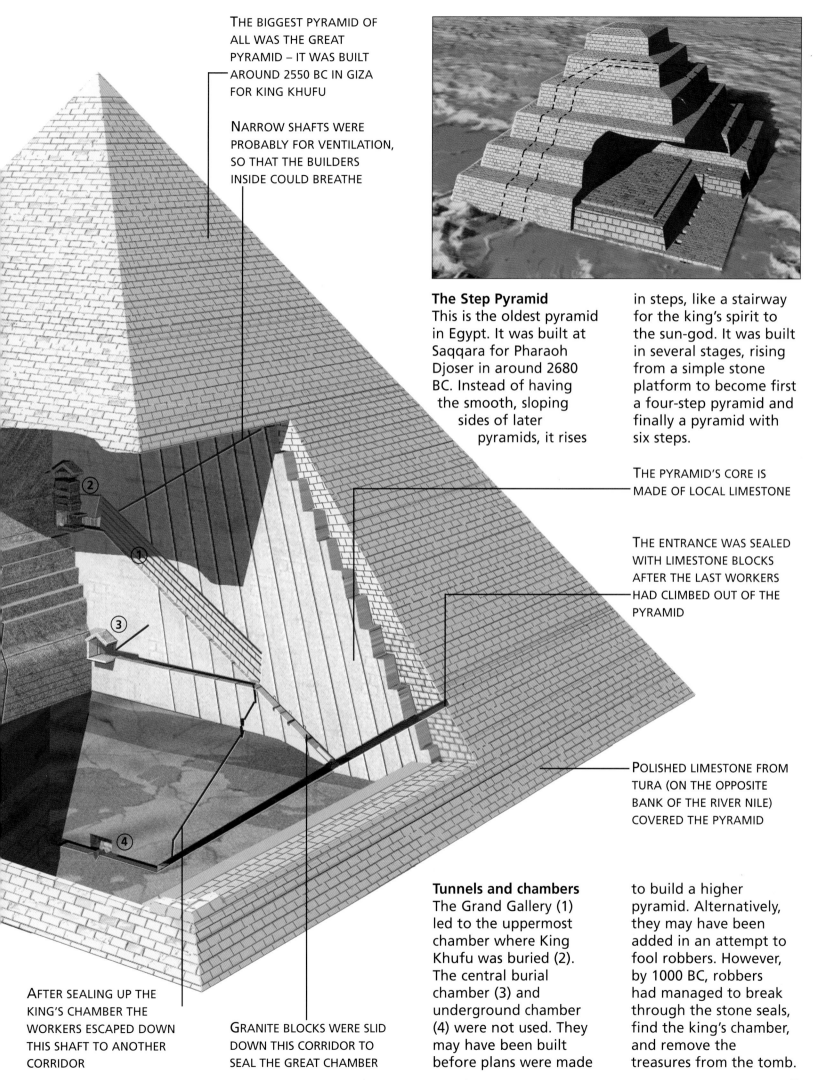

THE BIGGEST PYRAMID OF ALL WAS THE GREAT PYRAMID – IT WAS BUILT AROUND 2550 BC IN GIZA FOR KING KHUFU

NARROW SHAFTS WERE PROBABLY FOR VENTILATION, SO THAT THE BUILDERS INSIDE COULD BREATHE

The Step Pyramid

This is the oldest pyramid in Egypt. It was built at Saqqara for Pharaoh Djoser in around 2680 BC. Instead of having the smooth, sloping sides of later pyramids, it rises in steps, like a stairway for the king's spirit to the sun-god. It was built in several stages, rising from a simple stone platform to become first a four-step pyramid and finally a pyramid with six steps.

THE PYRAMID'S CORE IS MADE OF LOCAL LIMESTONE

THE ENTRANCE WAS SEALED WITH LIMESTONE BLOCKS AFTER THE LAST WORKERS HAD CLIMBED OUT OF THE PYRAMID

POLISHED LIMESTONE FROM TURA (ON THE OPPOSITE BANK OF THE RIVER NILE) COVERED THE PYRAMID

AFTER SEALING UP THE KING'S CHAMBER THE WORKERS ESCAPED DOWN THIS SHAFT TO ANOTHER CORRIDOR

GRANITE BLOCKS WERE SLID DOWN THIS CORRIDOR TO SEAL THE GREAT CHAMBER

Tunnels and chambers

The Grand Gallery (1) led to the uppermost chamber where King Khufu was buried (2). The central burial chamber (3) and underground chamber (4) were not used. They may have been built before plans were made to build a higher pyramid. Alternatively, they may have been added in an attempt to fool robbers. However, by 1000 BC, robbers had managed to break through the stone seals, find the king's chamber, and remove the treasures from the tomb.

Greek Temple

THE MOST famous temple in Greece is the Parthenon, on the Acropolis (a great outcrop of rock in Athens). The Parthenon was built in the 5th century BC and dedicated to Athena, the goddess of Athens. The temple is built of white marble, quarried at Mount Pentelicon, some 13 kilometres from the site. Each block was cut to size at the quarry. The smaller blocks were piled on carts and taken to the Acropolis; larger stones were rolled or dragged on sledges. Masons and sculptors at the site trimmed and carved the stones before they were put in position. Workers put up wooden scaffolding and used simple cranes, winches, and levers to lift the heavy stones into place. No mortar was used in the building – the Greeks developed a system of metal clamps to hold the blocks together.

Roof tiles
The tiles on the Parthenon's roof were made of a fine pale marble from the Greek island of Paros. Cut thin, this marble let through some natural light.

DECORATIVE FINIALS MARKED THE RIDGE AND CORNERS OF THE SLOPING ROOF

THE FRIEZE ABOVE THE COLUMNS IS MADE UP OF CARVED RELIEFS AND BLANK PANELS

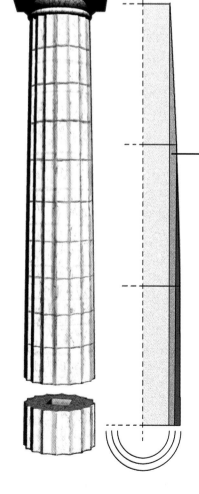

A SERIES OF CARVED RELIEFS RUNNING ROUND THE TEMPLE SHOWS SCENES FROM GREEK MYTHOLOGY

THIS ARCHITECT'S DRAWING SHOWS HOW THE COLUMNS TAPERED NEAR THE TOP TO DRAW THE EYE UPWARD

THE TEMPLE PLATFORM RISES A FEW CENTIMETRES IN THE MIDDLE, SO THAT IT APPEARS PERFECTLY FLAT FROM A DISTANCE

THE PARTHENON RESTS ON THE FOUNDATIONS OF AN EARLIER TEMPLE

Column construction
Each column is made up of eleven drum-like sections. The builders fixed wooden sockets in the middle of the drums, and pushed iron rods through the sockets to join the drums together. They hollowed out the surfaces slightly, to create a vacuum which pulled the drums together.

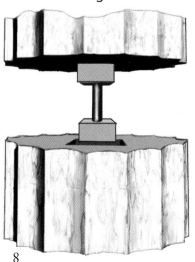

Doric design
The Parthenon is built in the Doric style. Its columns each have twenty flutes, but are otherwise very plain. At the top, each column ends in a square stone, called the abacus, above a plain round stone, the capital. Doric columns have no separate base and rest directly on the temple platform.

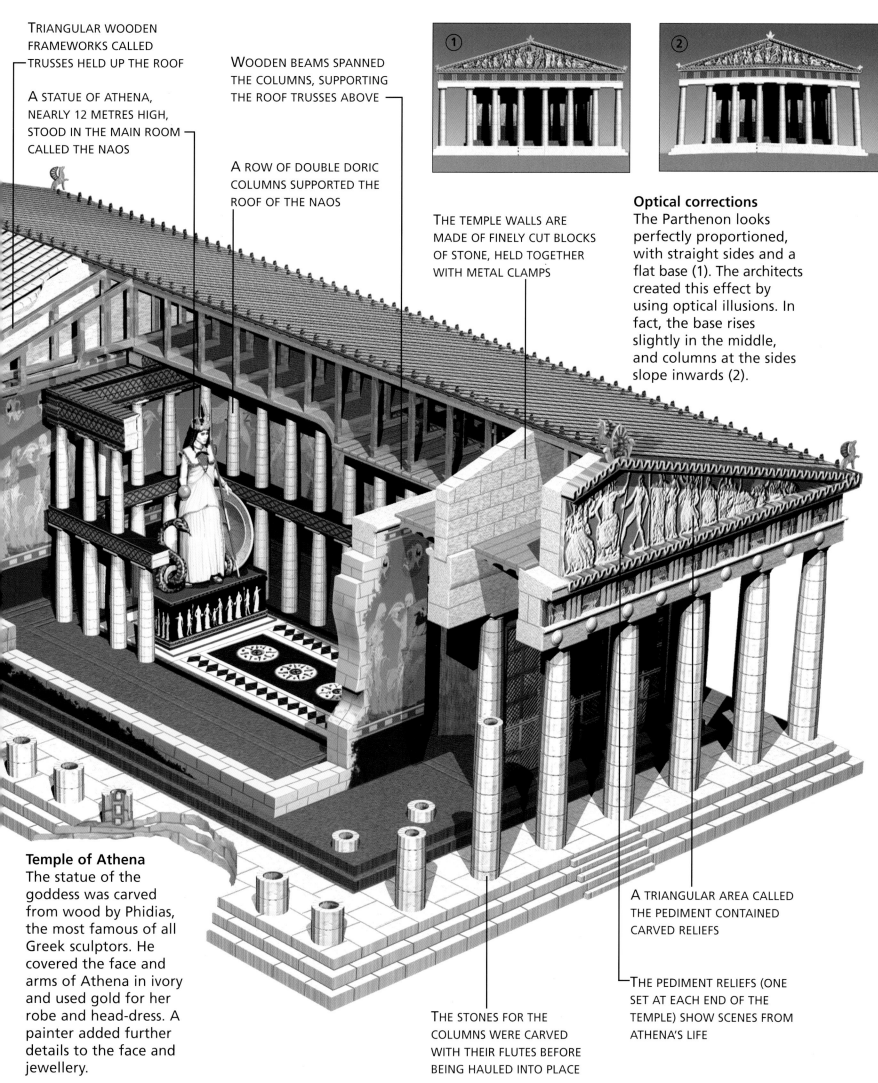

TRIANGULAR WOODEN FRAMEWORKS CALLED TRUSSES HELD UP THE ROOF

A STATUE OF ATHENA, NEARLY 12 METRES HIGH, STOOD IN THE MAIN ROOM CALLED THE NAOS

WOODEN BEAMS SPANNED THE COLUMNS, SUPPORTING THE ROOF TRUSSES ABOVE

A ROW OF DOUBLE DORIC COLUMNS SUPPORTED THE ROOF OF THE NAOS

THE TEMPLE WALLS ARE MADE OF FINELY CUT BLOCKS OF STONE, HELD TOGETHER WITH METAL CLAMPS

Optical corrections
The Parthenon looks perfectly proportioned, with straight sides and a flat base (1). The architects created this effect by using optical illusions. In fact, the base rises slightly in the middle, and columns at the sides slope inwards (2).

Temple of Athena
The statue of the goddess was carved from wood by Phidias, the most famous of all Greek sculptors. He covered the face and arms of Athena in ivory and used gold for her robe and head-dress. A painter added further details to the face and jewellery.

A TRIANGULAR AREA CALLED THE PEDIMENT CONTAINED CARVED RELIEFS

THE PEDIMENT RELIEFS (ONE SET AT EACH END OF THE TEMPLE) SHOW SCENES FROM ATHENA'S LIFE

THE STONES FOR THE COLUMNS WERE CARVED WITH THEIR FLUTES BEFORE BEING HAULED INTO PLACE

9

Colosseum

MOST ROMAN cities had amphitheatres, huge buildings where entertainments were staged. One of the greatest of these was the Colosseum in Rome. The building was begun in AD 72 to stage contests involving trained fighters called gladiators, combats between prisoners and wild animals, and boxing matches. To create such a huge building (about 49 metres high and 190 metres across), the Romans needed all their skill in stoneworking, bricklaying, and the use of concrete, then a fairly new material. Massive foundations supported the stone walls and marble seats. The central stage was a wooden floor covered with sand, and the Latin word for sand, *harena*, gave the arena its name. The builders also waterproofed the arena, and on one occasion it was flooded and a full-scale sea battle was staged.

POLES TO SUPPORT THE AWNING FITTED INTO HOLES CUT IN THE STONEWORK ALL AROUND THE TOP OF THE BUILDING

A CANVAS AWNING (COVER) STRETCHED ACROSS THE TOP OF THE COLOSSEUM. IT WAS PROBABLY DESIGNED TO SHADE THE SPECTATORS

A TRAPDOOR ENABLED THE LIONS TO WALK UP TO THE ARENA

CAGES COULD BE OPENED BY ROPES PULLED FROM BELOW

Under construction
Roman builders used simple hoists, cranes, and winches to haul heavy stone blocks up the side of the Colosseum. These devices were made by carpenters, who also made scaffolding and the temporary structures, called centring, that supported the arches and vaulting before the concrete set.

Lifting the animals
To protect their keepers, the wild animals were put in iron cages. When the time came for the creatures to enter the arena, men raised the cage using ropes and a simple wooden winch.

Then the cage door was opened using another rope. This allowed the animals only one escape route – up a ramp, through a trapdoor, and into the arena. Winches were also used to raise stage scenery.

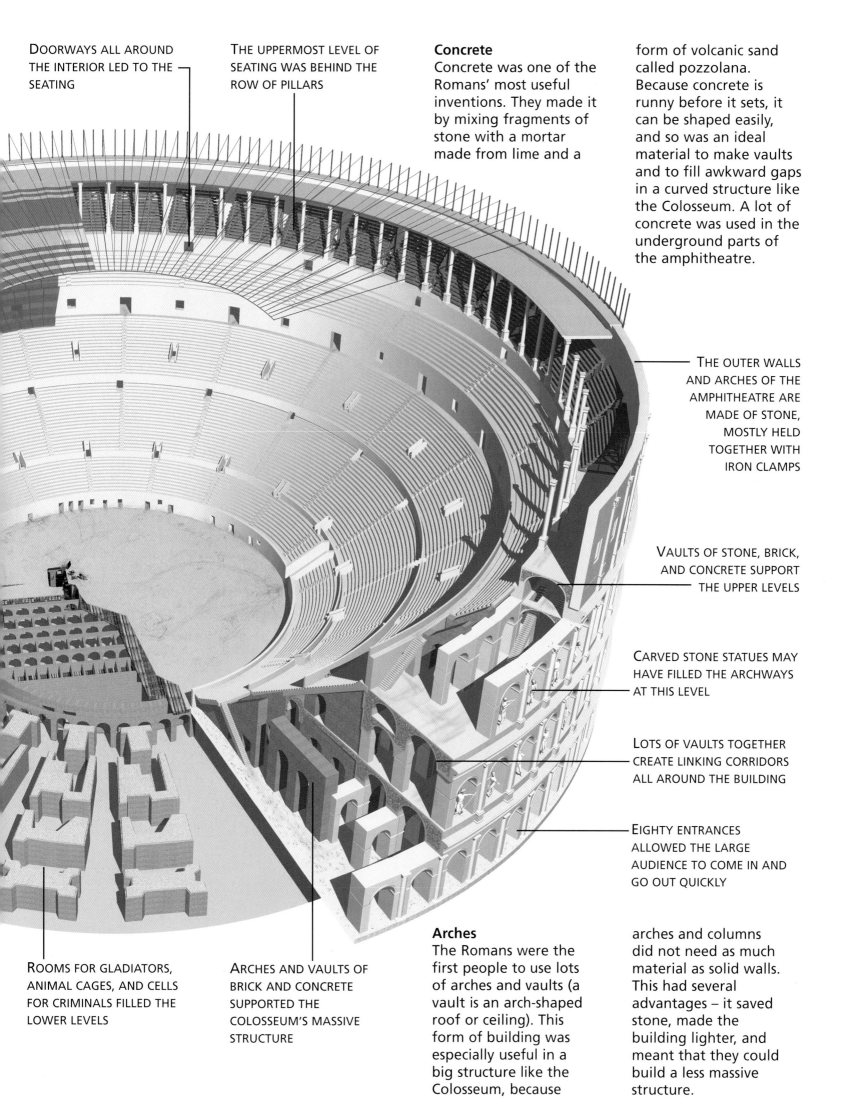

DOORWAYS ALL AROUND THE INTERIOR LED TO THE SEATING

THE UPPERMOST LEVEL OF SEATING WAS BEHIND THE ROW OF PILLARS

Concrete

Concrete was one of the Romans' most useful inventions. They made it by mixing fragments of stone with a mortar made from lime and a form of volcanic sand called pozzolana. Because concrete is runny before it sets, it can be shaped easily, and so was an ideal material to make vaults and to fill awkward gaps in a curved structure like the Colosseum. A lot of concrete was used in the underground parts of the amphitheatre.

THE OUTER WALLS AND ARCHES OF THE AMPHITHEATRE ARE MADE OF STONE, MOSTLY HELD TOGETHER WITH IRON CLAMPS

VAULTS OF STONE, BRICK, AND CONCRETE SUPPORT THE UPPER LEVELS

CARVED STONE STATUES MAY HAVE FILLED THE ARCHWAYS AT THIS LEVEL

LOTS OF VAULTS TOGETHER CREATE LINKING CORRIDORS ALL AROUND THE BUILDING

EIGHTY ENTRANCES ALLOWED THE LARGE AUDIENCE TO COME IN AND GO OUT QUICKLY

ROOMS FOR GLADIATORS, ANIMAL CAGES, AND CELLS FOR CRIMINALS FILLED THE LOWER LEVELS

ARCHES AND VAULTS OF BRICK AND CONCRETE SUPPORTED THE COLOSSEUM'S MASSIVE STRUCTURE

Arches

The Romans were the first people to use lots of arches and vaults (a vault is an arch-shaped roof or ceiling). This form of building was especially useful in a big structure like the Colosseum, because arches and columns did not need as much material as solid walls. This had several advantages – it saved stone, made the building lighter, and meant that they could build a less massive structure.

Roman Baths

IN THE HEART of ancient Rome were the great public baths, such as the Baths of the emperor Trajan which opened in AD 109 (*right*). These buildings were important because few Roman homes had their own bath. So people went to the city baths, where they moved from one room to another, starting in a cool pool, gradually building up to a sweltering heat, and finishing with a cold plunge. The baths were also social centres. People went there to gossip, read, do business deals, and exercise. The great baths were some of the Romans' most impressive buildings. Their huge, marble-lined halls were built in the classical style, adapted from the ancient Greeks. Behind the scenes was a maze of passages leading to the furnaces, as well as the ingenious heating systems, tanks, tubes, and hollow walls, that Roman engineers invented.

Hypocaust

The Romans invented an underfloor heating system called a hypocaust. They made a space by raising the floor up on short brick columns. This space was heated by a fire and the hot air warmed the floor. The walls were also heated in this way.

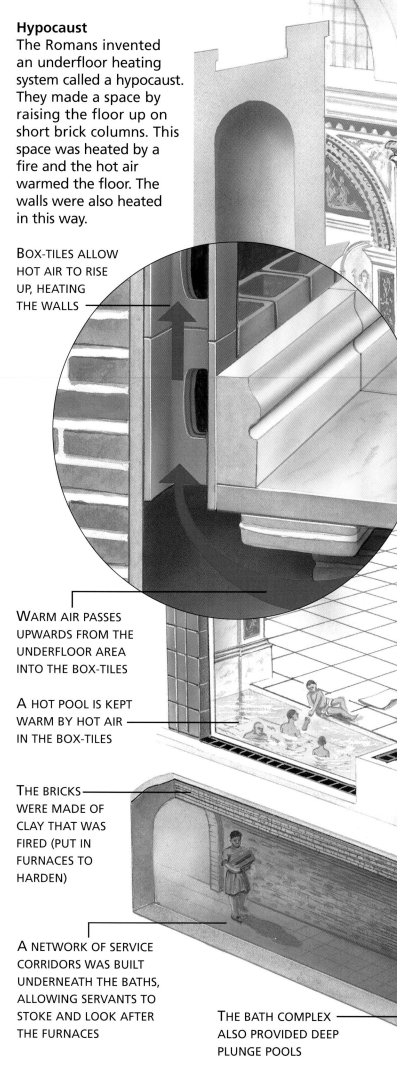

BOX-TILES ALLOW HOT AIR TO RISE UP, HEATING THE WALLS

WARM AIR PASSES UPWARDS FROM THE UNDERFLOOR AREA INTO THE BOX-TILES

A HOT POOL IS KEPT WARM BY HOT AIR IN THE BOX-TILES

THE BRICKS WERE MADE OF CLAY THAT WAS FIRED (PUT IN FURNACES TO HARDEN)

A NETWORK OF SERVICE CORRIDORS WAS BUILT UNDERNEATH THE BATHS, ALLOWING SERVANTS TO STOKE AND LOOK AFTER THE FURNACES

THE BATH COMPLEX ALSO PROVIDED DEEP PLUNGE POOLS

City layout

Trajan's baths (1) were near the centre of Rome, in the area where the Romans went for their entertainment. Nearby were the Colosseum (2) and the Ludus Magnus (3), where gladiators were trained. All around, the straight streets are flanked by classical-style buildings, many of which are built around courtyards, which is typical in Rome.

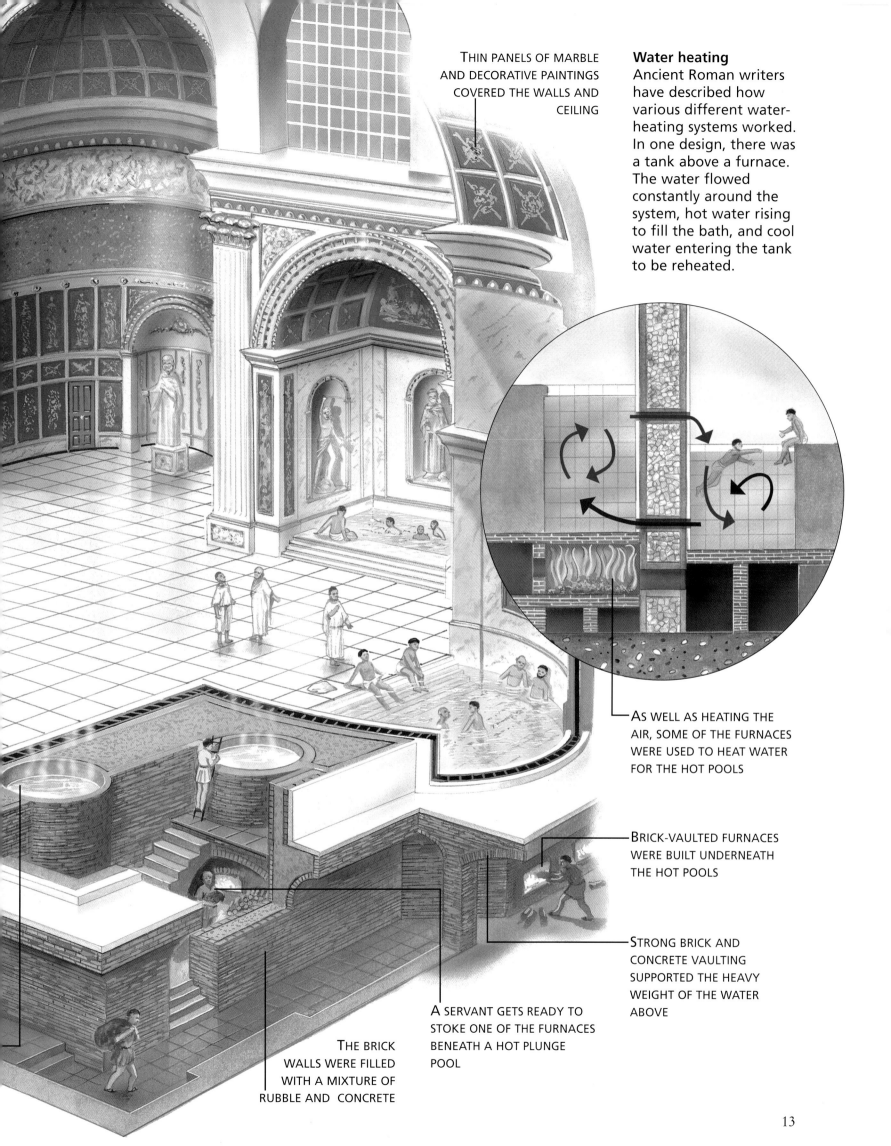

THIN PANELS OF MARBLE AND DECORATIVE PAINTINGS COVERED THE WALLS AND CEILING

Water heating
Ancient Roman writers have described how various different water-heating systems worked. In one design, there was a tank above a furnace. The water flowed constantly around the system, hot water rising to fill the bath, and cool water entering the tank to be reheated.

AS WELL AS HEATING THE AIR, SOME OF THE FURNACES WERE USED TO HEAT WATER FOR THE HOT POOLS

BRICK-VAULTED FURNACES WERE BUILT UNDERNEATH THE HOT POOLS

STRONG BRICK AND CONCRETE VAULTING SUPPORTED THE HEAVY WEIGHT OF THE WATER ABOVE

A SERVANT GETS READY TO STOKE ONE OF THE FURNACES BENEATH A HOT PLUNGE POOL

THE BRICK WALLS WERE FILLED WITH A MIXTURE OF RUBBLE AND CONCRETE

13

Medieval Castle

THE CASTLES of the Middle Ages were designed for strength. Their thick stone walls were built to withstand a pounding from battering-rams. Their towers and wall walks provided firing platforms for defending archers. Their gates could hold back the strongest enemy. Some of the most impressive of all castles were built by the English king Edward I (1272–1307), in his campaign to conquer and rule Wales. Conwy (*right*), in North Wales, is one of the best preserved. It was used as a military base, government headquarters, and home for the king. In order to withstand a long siege, it had its own water supply, large storerooms for food, and room for a small army.

ROUND TOWERS GIVE DEFENDERS A GOOD VIEW OF THE COUNTRYSIDE

TINY WINDOWS ARE A DIFFICULT TARGET FOR ENEMY ARROWS

A CORNER TOWER CONTAINS ROOMS FOR THE ROYAL HOUSEHOLD, AND A SMALL PRIVATE CHAPEL

THE KITCHEN TOWER CONTAINED STOREROOMS FOR FOOD AND DRINK TO SUPPLY THE NEARBY KITCHEN

THIS WALL FORMS PART OF THE TOWN'S DEFENCES

THIS CORNER TOWER PROVIDES LIVING ACCOMMODATION FOR THE CONSTABLE, WHO TOOK COMMAND OF THE CASTLE WHEN THE KING WAS ABSENT

THE GATEHOUSE WITH TWIN TOWERS, DRAWBRIDGE, AND PORTCULLIS IS THE MOST STRONGLY GUARDED PART OF THE CASTLE

A DITCH PROVIDES FURTHER PROTECTION

Entrance defences
Visitors entered the castle over a drawbridge. There were two ways of barring the way to an enemy. First, the draw-bridge (*above, left*) could be raised, using a winch turned by two men on the upper floor of the gatehouse. Second, rising and falling gates, called portcullises (*above, right*) could be lowered. These strong gates were made of wooden beams reinforced with iron. They were also moved with winches, which the guards controlled by pulling on wooden poles. Many castles had a pair of portcullises, which could be lowered one after the other to trap the enemy inside.

THE KING'S TOWER CONTAINS PRIVATE ROOMS FOR THE ROYAL FAMILY; THE MAIN ROOMS HAVE LARGE STONE FIREPLACES

CRENELLATIONS (BATTLEMENTS) PROTECT DEFENDING ARCHERS

THE PRISON TOWER CONTAINS A BASEMENT DUNGEON, ENTERED THROUGH A TRAPDOOR IN THE FLOOR ABOVE

Courtyard and chambers
Anyone entering the castle came in through the gatehouse into the barbican (1), or entrance area. Next they came to the outer court (2), the public area of the castle. Here were the stables, kitchen (3), and chapel (4). At the heart of the outer court was the hall (5), where everyone ate, and where business was discussed. Beyond was the inner court (6). This was reserved for the king and his household. As well as the royal living rooms, it housed a presence chamber (7), where the king received important visitors.

THE CASTLE IS BUILT OF STONE QUARRIED FROM NEARBY

CONICAL ROOFS ARE COVERED WITH LEAD

MACHICOLATIONS (HOLES IN THE OVERHANGING WALL WALK) ALLOW DEFENDERS TO POUR HOT WATER OR BOILING OIL ON ENEMIES BENEATH

BEDROCK (NATURALLY OCCURRING ROCK) MAKES SOLID FOUNDATIONS FOR THE CASTLE'S MASSIVE WALLS

THE BARBICAN GIVES EXTRA PROTECTION TO THE CASTLE ENTRANCE

Cathedral

THE CATHEDRALS of Europe are the most amazing buildings that survive from the Middle Ages. The most magnificent, such as the cathedral of Notre Dame in Paris (*right*), are built in the Gothic style, which combines pointed arches, high, vaulted ceilings, and large windows. The medieval builders needed great skill to create these structures. The huge windows meant that there was very little stonework to support the heavy ceilings. So the builders invented the flying buttress, an arched wall support, to help take the weight. The result was stunning, with everything – the pointed arches, the towers and spires, the high ceilings – designed to make the visitor look up, as if towards heaven. By adding richly coloured, stained glass and many sculptures of saints and scenes from the Bible, an image of heaven on earth was created.

Gargoyles
Although the carvings on the inside of the cathedral show sacred subjects, some of those outside portray animals, devils, and mythical beasts. The most grotesque of these sculptures, high up on the building's walls, are called gargoyles.

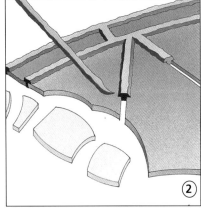

Stained glass
The glass-maker mixed coloured chemicals into the glass. Then he heated the glass and blew a piece into a bubble, cut this along its length and heated it again to flatten it out (1). Pieces of glass were joined with lead strips (2) to make a panel (3).

MASONS (STONE WORKERS) SHAPED THE STONE BY HAND

GARGOYLES, SOME CONTAINING RAINWATER SPOUTS, STICK OUT FROM TOWER

TALL LOUVRED (SLATTED) OPENINGS ALLOW THE SOUND OF THE BELLS TO BE HEARD

BUTTRESSES HELP TO CARRY THE WEIGHT OF THE TOWER

THE STAINED GLASS WHEEL WINDOW IS 13 METRES IN DIAMETER

A ROW OF STATUES OF THE KINGS OF FRANCE STRETCHES RIGHT ACROSS THE WEST FRONT

CARVED STATUES OF CHARACTERS FROM THE BIBLE DECORATE THE SIDES OF THE DOORWAYS

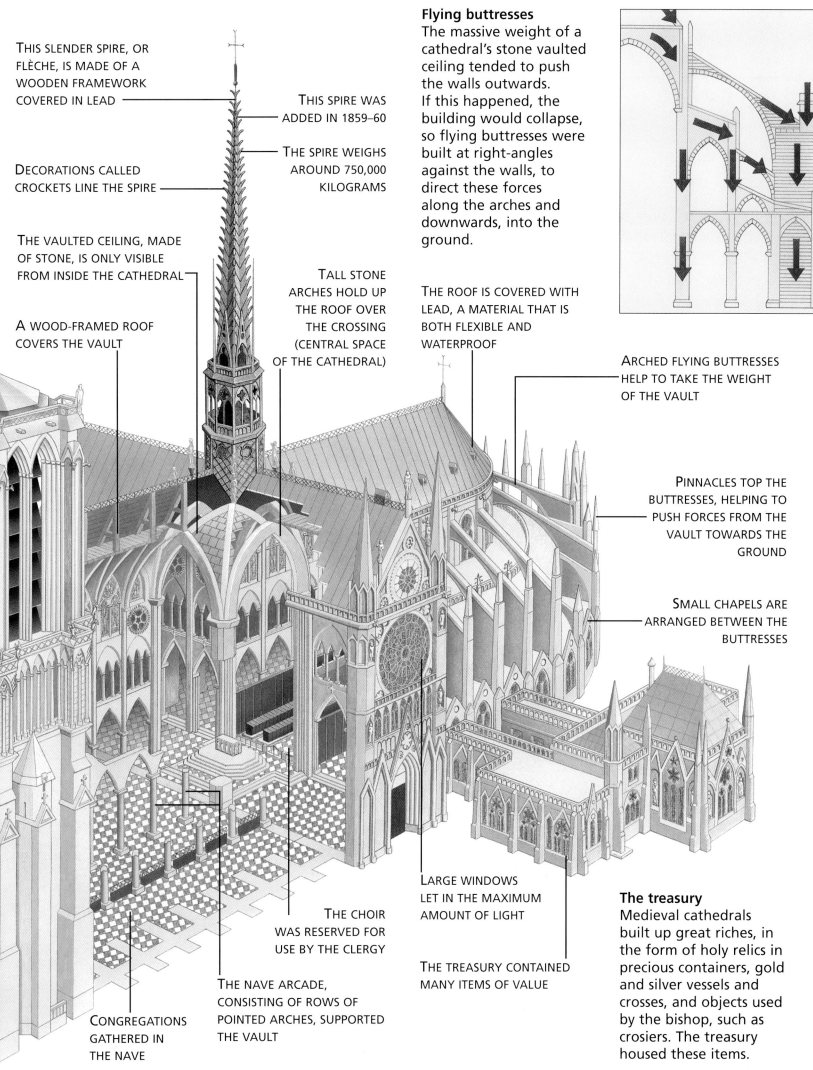

THIS SLENDER SPIRE, OR FLÈCHE, IS MADE OF A WOODEN FRAMEWORK COVERED IN LEAD

THIS SPIRE WAS ADDED IN 1859–60

THE SPIRE WEIGHS AROUND 750,000 KILOGRAMS

DECORATIONS CALLED CROCKETS LINE THE SPIRE

THE VAULTED CEILING, MADE OF STONE, IS ONLY VISIBLE FROM INSIDE THE CATHEDRAL

A WOOD-FRAMED ROOF COVERS THE VAULT

TALL STONE ARCHES HOLD UP THE ROOF OVER THE CROSSING (CENTRAL SPACE OF THE CATHEDRAL)

Flying buttresses
The massive weight of a cathedral's stone vaulted ceiling tended to push the walls outwards. If this happened, the building would collapse, so flying buttresses were built at right-angles against the walls, to direct these forces along the arches and downwards, into the ground.

THE ROOF IS COVERED WITH LEAD, A MATERIAL THAT IS BOTH FLEXIBLE AND WATERPROOF

ARCHED FLYING BUTTRESSES HELP TO TAKE THE WEIGHT OF THE VAULT

PINNACLES TOP THE BUTTRESSES, HELPING TO PUSH FORCES FROM THE VAULT TOWARDS THE GROUND

SMALL CHAPELS ARE ARRANGED BETWEEN THE BUTTRESSES

LARGE WINDOWS LET IN THE MAXIMUM AMOUNT OF LIGHT

THE CHOIR WAS RESERVED FOR USE BY THE CLERGY

THE NAVE ARCADE, CONSISTING OF ROWS OF POINTED ARCHES, SUPPORTED THE VAULT

CONGREGATIONS GATHERED IN THE NAVE

THE TREASURY CONTAINED MANY ITEMS OF VALUE

The treasury
Medieval cathedrals built up great riches, in the form of holy relics in precious containers, gold and silver vessels and crosses, and objects used by the bishop, such as crosiers. The treasury housed these items.

Pagodas

PAGODAS ARE tall, tower-like buildings that usually form part of a Buddhist temple or shrine. Pagodas were first built in India and spread with Buddhism to China and Japan. Some of the most beautiful pagodas are in Japan. Built of wood, they display the great skill of carpenters working hundreds of years ago. The carpenters had to invent special joints and brackets, and had to learn how to find, prepare, and carry the large timbers that were used. The structures they built have lasted well – some have even withstood earthquakes. The builders also had to understand the symbolism of their Buddhist faith. A pagoda was a symbol of the sacred mountain that leads to heaven, and its storeys, which get smaller the higher they go, are meant to suggest the soul rising until it reaches infinity.

Eaves bracketing

The overhanging roofs of pagodas like the Eastern Pagoda (*right*) need to be held up at the edges. Japanese carpenters invented a clever system of brackets to do this (*see below*). The brackets are timber supports that branch out, like a tree.

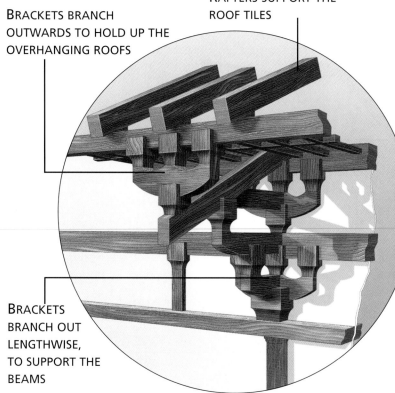

RAFTERS SUPPORT THE ROOF TILES

BRACKETS BRANCH OUTWARDS TO HOLD UP THE OVERHANGING ROOFS

BRACKETS BRANCH OUT LENGTHWISE, TO SUPPORT THE BEAMS

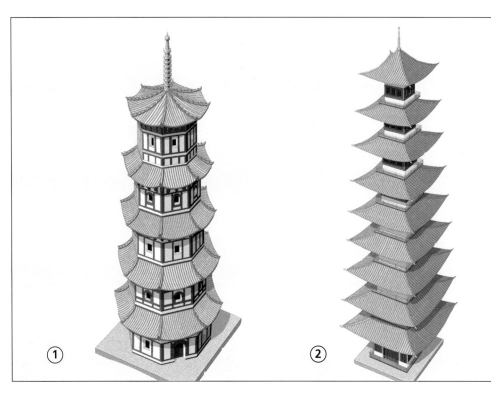

① ②

Pagodas in China

Some Chinese pagodas are built of stone (1). This example, in Quanzhou, is octagonal. Its stonework, with brackets under the eaves (roof edges), copies the structure of wooden pagodas. Others, like the nine-storey example from Shanghai (2) are built of wood with some of the details made of clay baked in a kiln.

The Buddha

Buddhist pagodas and temples usually contain statues of the Buddha, the founder of the faith. These can be huge images, cast from bronze. They are so large that the temples had to be built around them.

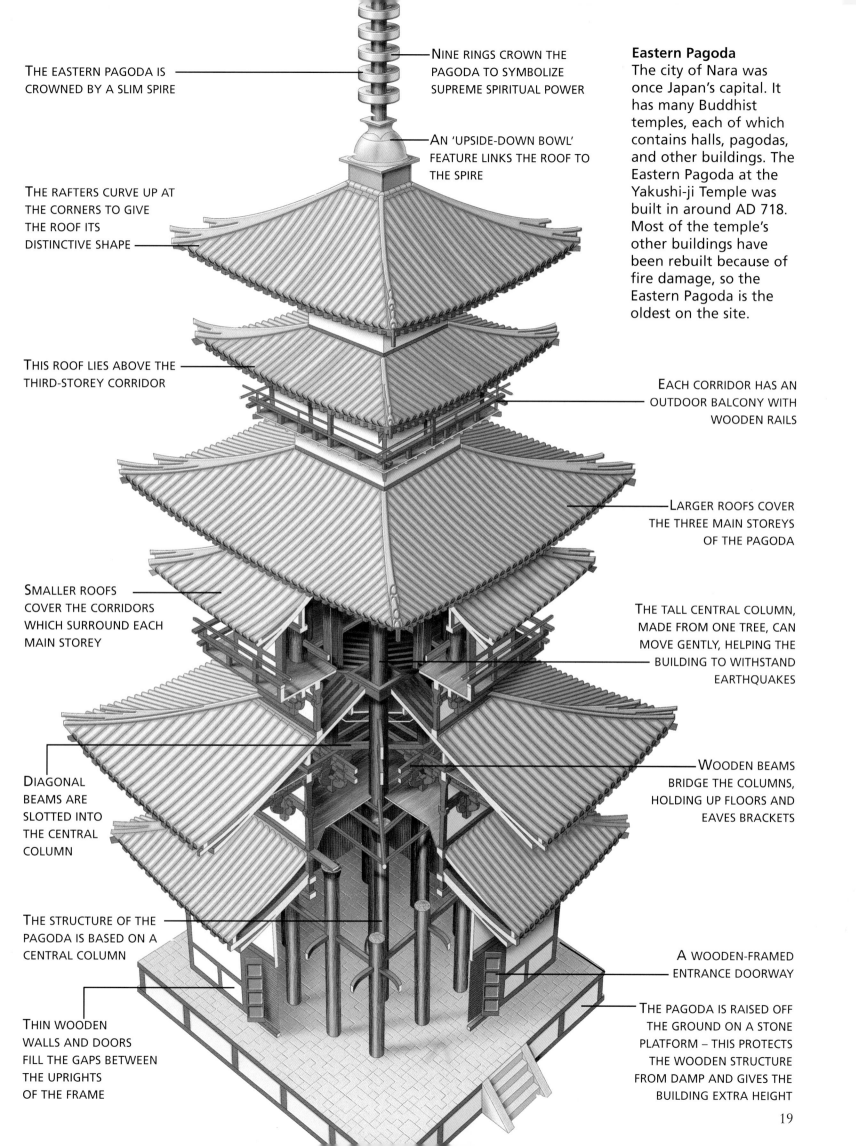

THE EASTERN PAGODA IS CROWNED BY A SLIM SPIRE

NINE RINGS CROWN THE PAGODA TO SYMBOLIZE SUPREME SPIRITUAL POWER

AN 'UPSIDE-DOWN BOWL' FEATURE LINKS THE ROOF TO THE SPIRE

THE RAFTERS CURVE UP AT THE CORNERS TO GIVE THE ROOF ITS DISTINCTIVE SHAPE

THIS ROOF LIES ABOVE THE THIRD-STOREY CORRIDOR

SMALLER ROOFS COVER THE CORRIDORS WHICH SURROUND EACH MAIN STOREY

DIAGONAL BEAMS ARE SLOTTED INTO THE CENTRAL COLUMN

THE STRUCTURE OF THE PAGODA IS BASED ON A CENTRAL COLUMN

THIN WOODEN WALLS AND DOORS FILL THE GAPS BETWEEN THE UPRIGHTS OF THE FRAME

Eastern Pagoda
The city of Nara was once Japan's capital. It has many Buddhist temples, each of which contains halls, pagodas, and other buildings. The Eastern Pagoda at the Yakushi-ji Temple was built in around AD 718. Most of the temple's other buildings have been rebuilt because of fire damage, so the Eastern Pagoda is the oldest on the site.

EACH CORRIDOR HAS AN OUTDOOR BALCONY WITH WOODEN RAILS

LARGER ROOFS COVER THE THREE MAIN STOREYS OF THE PAGODA

THE TALL CENTRAL COLUMN, MADE FROM ONE TREE, CAN MOVE GENTLY, HELPING THE BUILDING TO WITHSTAND EARTHQUAKES

WOODEN BEAMS BRIDGE THE COLUMNS, HOLDING UP FLOORS AND EAVES BRACKETS

A WOODEN-FRAMED ENTRANCE DOORWAY

THE PAGODA IS RAISED OFF THE GROUND ON A STONE PLATFORM – THIS PROTECTS THE WOODEN STRUCTURE FROM DAMP AND GIVES THE BUILDING EXTRA HEIGHT

19

Imperial Palace

CHINA'S capital city, Beijing, was rebuilt during the Ming Dynasty (1368–1644) with the Imperial Palace at its centre. More like a small town than a palace, this complex was soon nicknamed the 'Forbidden City', because only the emperor and those on imperial business were allowed through its gates. At its centre is the Hall of Supreme Harmony, the emperor's reception hall where he watched over important ceremonies (*right*). The hall's most striking feature is its overhanging roof. Everything about this roof is designed to show that it belongs to the emperor – its large size and two-storey structure are both signs that it is an imperial building. The rest of the hall is made of wood and consists of an elaborate frame of columns and beams.

Lion on guard
A large statue of a lion, cast from bronze, sits at the entrance to the Hall of Supreme Harmony. In China, the lion traditionally stands for energy, strength, and bravery, and so is a good symbol for an emperor and his power.

DECORATIVE TILES ON THE ROOF CORNERS PORTRAY MYTHICAL BEASTS

THE SPECIAL DOUBLE ROOF DESIGN WAS KEPT FOR THE MOST IMPORTANT BUILDINGS, SUCH AS THOSE USED BY THE EMPEROR

ROWS OF PAINTED WOODEN COLUMNS HOLD UP THE ROOF OF THE HALL OF SUPREME HARMONY

Forbidden City
The Hall of Supreme Harmony is at the heart of the city. The main halls are in a row along the city's central axis. Lesser buildings, such as the library, the workshops, and the palace kitchens, are arranged around the edges.

IN 1406, 200,000 WORKERS BEGAN TO BUILD THE FORBIDDEN CITY

THE FORBIDDEN CITY COVERS AN AREA OF AROUND 70 HECTARES

A WALL AND MOAT SURROUND THE PALACE

Key to the city map
(1) Meridian Gate;
(2) Gate of Supreme Harmony; (3) Hall of Supreme Harmony;
(4) Hall of Complete Harmony; (5) Hall of Preserving Harmony;
(6) Palace of Heavenly Purity; (7) Palace of Earthly Tranquillity; and
(8) River of Golden Water.

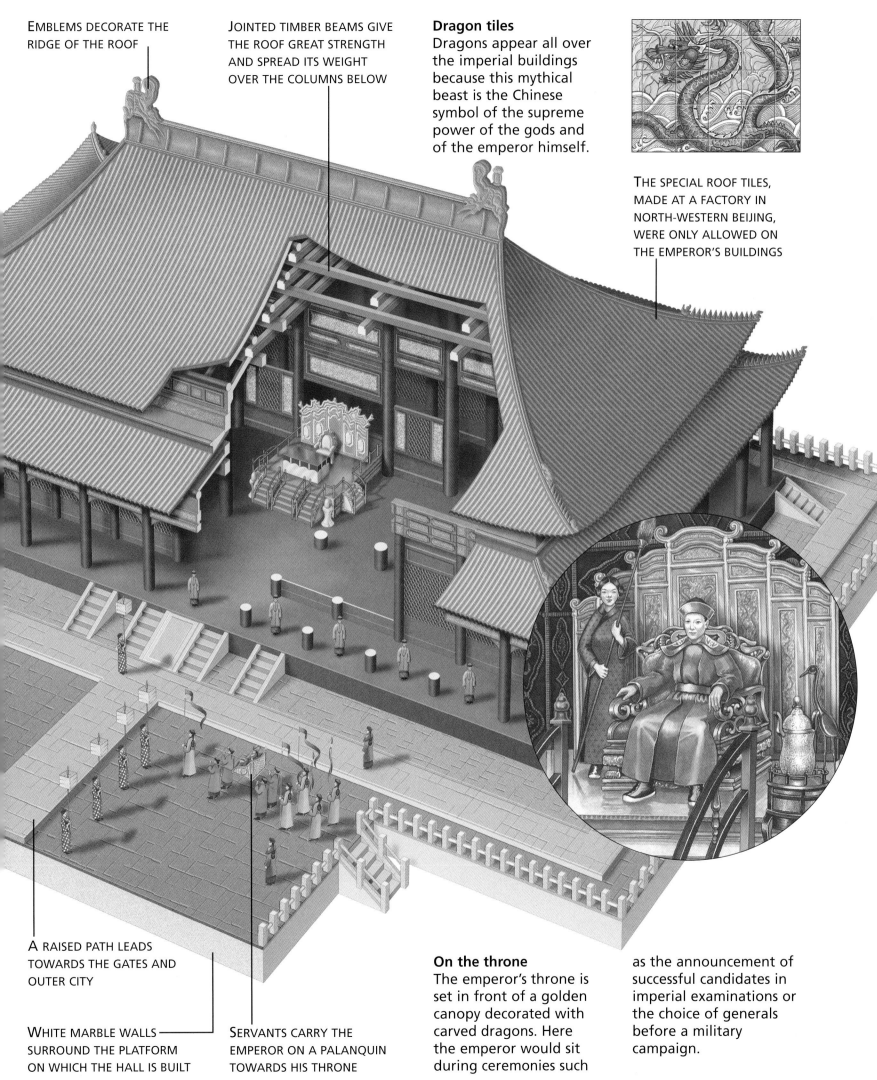

EMBLEMS DECORATE THE RIDGE OF THE ROOF

JOINTED TIMBER BEAMS GIVE THE ROOF GREAT STRENGTH AND SPREAD ITS WEIGHT OVER THE COLUMNS BELOW

Dragon tiles
Dragons appear all over the imperial buildings because this mythical beast is the Chinese symbol of the supreme power of the gods and of the emperor himself.

THE SPECIAL ROOF TILES, MADE AT A FACTORY IN NORTH-WESTERN BEIJING, WERE ONLY ALLOWED ON THE EMPEROR'S BUILDINGS

A RAISED PATH LEADS TOWARDS THE GATES AND OUTER CITY

WHITE MARBLE WALLS SURROUND THE PLATFORM ON WHICH THE HALL IS BUILT

SERVANTS CARRY THE EMPEROR ON A PALANQUIN TOWARDS HIS THRONE

On the throne
The emperor's throne is set in front of a golden canopy decorated with carved dragons. Here the emperor would sit during ceremonies such as the announcement of successful candidates in imperial examinations or the choice of generals before a military campaign.

Skyscrapers

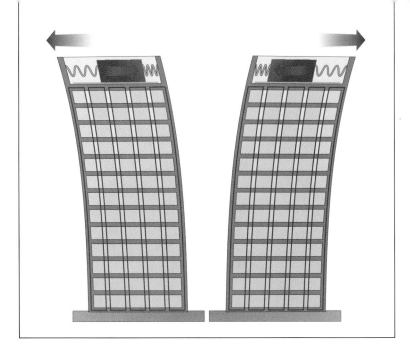

SKYSCRAPERS need to stand on a firm base or foundation. This is usually made of upright concrete or steel posts, called piles, which are driven into the ground. Above the piles, builders assemble a concrete raft or network of beams to spread the building's weight across the piles. The building is held together by its frame, a network of upright columns and horizontal beams, most often made of steel. To make the concrete parts of the skyscraper, such as floors, builders pour liquid concrete into wooden boxes, called formwork, which can be removed when the material has set. The outer layer or 'skin' of the building is called the cladding. It is quite thin and is usually made of metal (such as steel) and glass.

Dynamic dampers
Tall buildings in earthquake zones often need special protection. One solution is to fit a massive concrete block at the top of the skyscraper. The block floats on a film of oil, so that it can move, and is linked to the building's framework with huge springs. In an earthquake, as the earth vibrates, the building moves under the block, but the springs pull the structure back to its correct upright position.

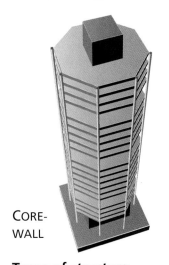

CORE-WALL

FRAMED-TUBE

TRUSSED

Types of structure
A core-wall skyscraper has a concrete core (*above*). Huge brackets called cantilevers stick out from the core to support the floors. Framed-tube towers (*above right*) are held together with a framework of steel columns and beams. For extra strength in high towers, a framed tube can be trussed (*right*), or strengthened with diagonal beams.

BEAMS SUPPORT THE FLOOR

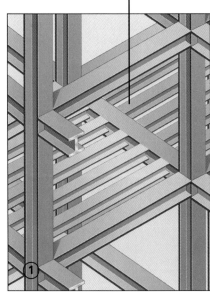

CORRUGATED METAL

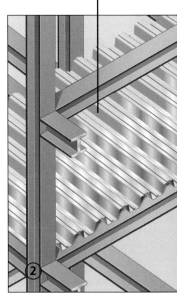

Floor construction
The steel beams (1) that criss-cross the skyscraper support the floor. Workers weld sheets of metal to the beams (2). The metal is corrugated, which makes it strong but keeps it light in weight. Lightweight concrete is poured on top of the corrugated metal, which sets to create a solid floor that is not too heavy (3). Floor coverings – tiles, carpets, or wooden strips – are laid on top of the concrete. In many buildings, a space is left under the floor to take cables for electricity, telephones, and computers.

Cranes

A crane is quite a simple machine with a lifting mechanism that pulls a cable over a long, movable arm or jib. The cranes used to build skyscrapers have a climbing mechanism. This consists of a powerful jack to lift the crane, and sets of clamps which keep it attached to the building's framework.

THE CANARY WHARF TOWER IN LONDON IS A FRAMED-TUBE SKYSCRAPER

THE COLUMNS AND BEAMS ARE ARRANGED CLOSE TOGETHER, FOR MAXIMUM STRENGTH

STEEL AND GLASS CLADDING COVERS THE SURFACE OF THE BUILDING

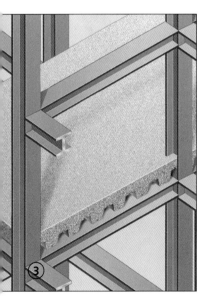

A CONCRETE RAFT ABOUT 5 METRES THICK PROVIDES THE SKYSCRAPER'S FOUNDATION

EACH OF THE 222 PILES MEASURES 1.5 METRES ACROSS

THE PILES ARE DRIVEN 18 METRES INTO THE SOIL, TO ANCHOR THE BUILDING IN PLACE

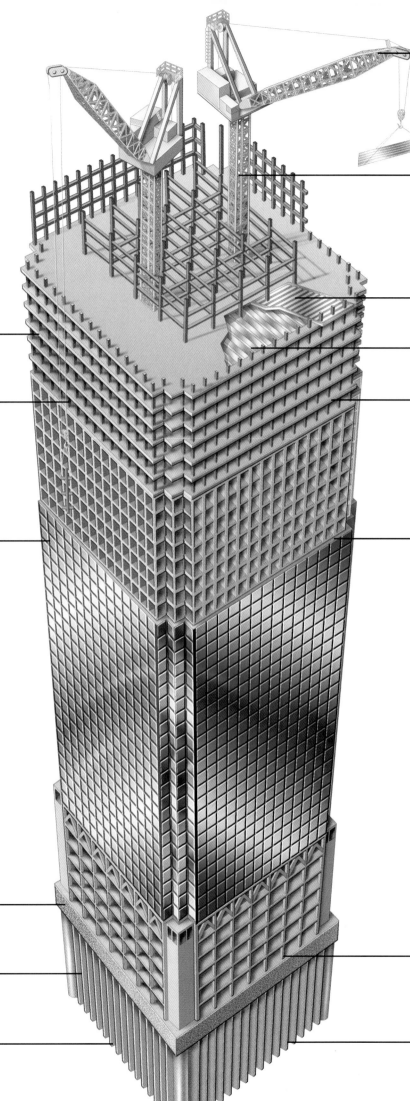

THE JIB OF THE CRANE STICKS OUT WELL BEYOND THE FACE OF THE BUILDING

THE CRANE'S TOWER CAN 'CLIMB' UP THE FRAME-WORK, RISING WITH THE GROWING SKYSCRAPER

CORRUGATED (RIDGED) METAL DECKING FORMS THE FLOOR

THE FLOOR DECKING IS SUPPORTED BY STEEL BEAMS

THE FRAMEWORK IS HELD TOGETHER WITH LARGE STEEL BOLTS

THE EDGE OF A FLOOR PROVIDES AN ANCHOR POINT FOR THE CLADDING

Under construction

Building a skyscraper is a complex process. The architect draws up some plans with the help of specialists, such as a civil engineer who makes sure that the proposed structure is sound. Next, the site has to be cleared, piles driven, and foundations laid. Then the skyscraper grows as the framework is built, followed by the outer cladding, and then the services, such as wiring and drainage.

UPRIGHT COLUMNS ARE FIXED TO THE CONCRETE RAFT

PILES PASS THROUGH SOFT UPPER SOIL SO THAT THEIR BASES ARE DEEP ENOUGH TO REACH STRONG, SUPPORTING SOIL

Hong Kong Skyscraper

TOWERING over our crowded cities, skyscrapers pack huge areas of floor space into a tiny area of land. The famous Hong Kong Bank, opened in 1985, is one of many impressive modern office blocks crammed into the small space available in the city of Hong Kong. Designed by British architect Norman Foster, it is 179 metres high and has 42 storeys. Its load-carrying steel framework is on the outside of the building. However, the carefully designed framework does not cover the building's sides and so allows plenty of light to pass through the windows into the offices and plazas inside. The frame has been coated with a thin layer of special cement so that it will not rust easily in the city air. The structure is similar to a framed-tube (*see page 22*), but includes new elements such as diagonal beams to help support its framework.

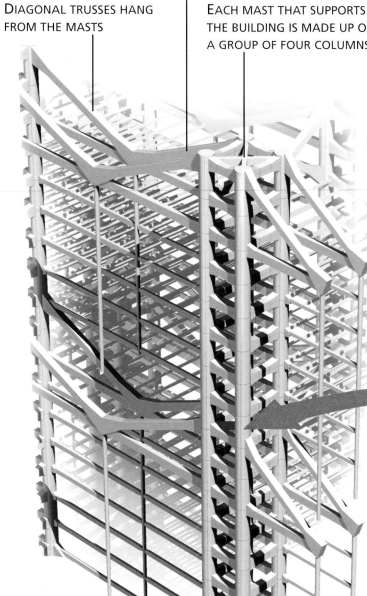

THE SKYSCRAPER'S STRUCTURE IS LIKE A SKELETON

DIAGONAL TRUSSES HANG FROM THE MASTS

EACH MAST THAT SUPPORTS THE BUILDING IS MADE UP OF A GROUP OF FOUR COLUMNS

UPRIGHT 'HANGERS' HOLD THE FLOOR BEAMS IN PLACE

THE MAIN ENTRANCE LEADS TO THE ATRIUM

THE LOOP OF CABLE IS WOUND BY AN ELECTRIC MOTOR

A COUNTERWEIGHT BALANCES THE LIFT CAR

THE LIFT CAR

Passenger lifts
A modern passenger lift is powered by an electric motor which moves a loop of steel cable attached to the lift car and its counterweight. There is an automatic breaking system that works if the lift begins to move too quickly. Guide rails stop the car swaying.

BUFFERS ABSORB SHOCK IF THE LIFT DROPS TOO FAR

The structure
The skyscraper is based on a 'skeleton' of steel tubes and beams. The 'backbone' of the building is provided by eight tall masts, each made up of four columns tied together with short cross-braces. Crossing the masts at five different levels are the long diagonal beams, called trusses, that give this skyscraper its special appearance. These trusses support the floors below, which are connected together by a series of upright beams, known as hangers.

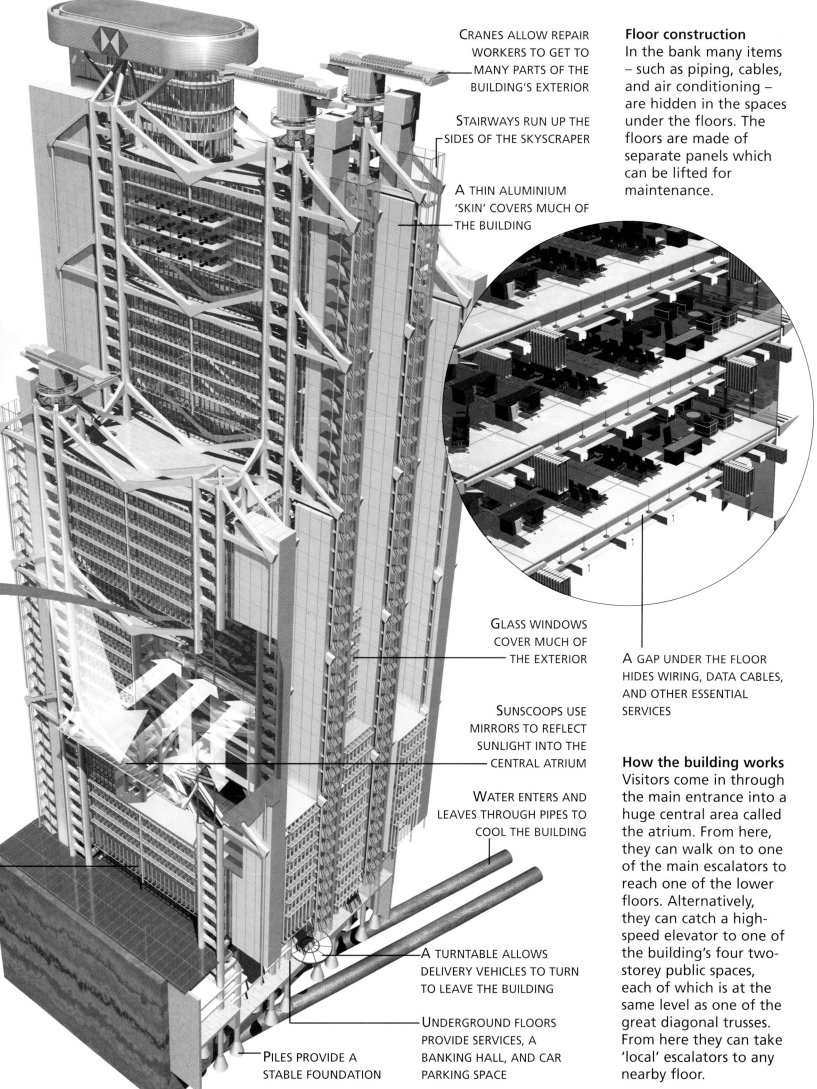

CRANES ALLOW REPAIR WORKERS TO GET TO MANY PARTS OF THE BUILDING'S EXTERIOR

STAIRWAYS RUN UP THE SIDES OF THE SKYSCRAPER

A THIN ALUMINIUM 'SKIN' COVERS MUCH OF THE BUILDING

Floor construction
In the bank many items – such as piping, cables, and air conditioning – are hidden in the spaces under the floors. The floors are made of separate panels which can be lifted for maintenance.

GLASS WINDOWS COVER MUCH OF THE EXTERIOR

A GAP UNDER THE FLOOR HIDES WIRING, DATA CABLES, AND OTHER ESSENTIAL SERVICES

SUNSCOOPS USE MIRRORS TO REFLECT SUNLIGHT INTO THE CENTRAL ATRIUM

How the building works
Visitors come in through the main entrance into a huge central area called the atrium. From here, they can walk on to one of the main escalators to reach one of the lower floors. Alternatively, they can catch a high-speed elevator to one of the building's four two-storey public spaces, each of which is at the same level as one of the great diagonal trusses. From here they can take 'local' escalators to any nearby floor.

WATER ENTERS AND LEAVES THROUGH PIPES TO COOL THE BUILDING

A TURNTABLE ALLOWS DELIVERY VEHICLES TO TURN TO LEAVE THE BUILDING

UNDERGROUND FLOORS PROVIDE SERVICES, A BANKING HALL, AND CAR PARKING SPACE

PILES PROVIDE A STABLE FOUNDATION

Opera House

SYDNEY'S OPERA House is one of the most dramatic buildings in the world. The original design was by the Danish architect Jørn Utzon, but when construction began in 1959, it became clear that Utzon had not worked out how his striking roof shapes could be built. The British engineering firm Ove Arup, and a group of Australian architects, helped solve the problem. The team worked out that the curves of the roof should be like sections of a globe. Then they developed a design for the roof's structure, made of a network of concrete pieces. Each piece was cast specially, before being lifted into place by tall cranes. Finally, the roofs were covered with gleaming ceramic tiles.

CAD
Computer-aided design (CAD) is now used widely by architects. It enables the architect to view the design from any angle (*below, left*), alter the design and add details (*below, right*) much more quickly than when drawing by hand. Computers can also be used to view the effects of wind and other loads without needing to make expensive models.

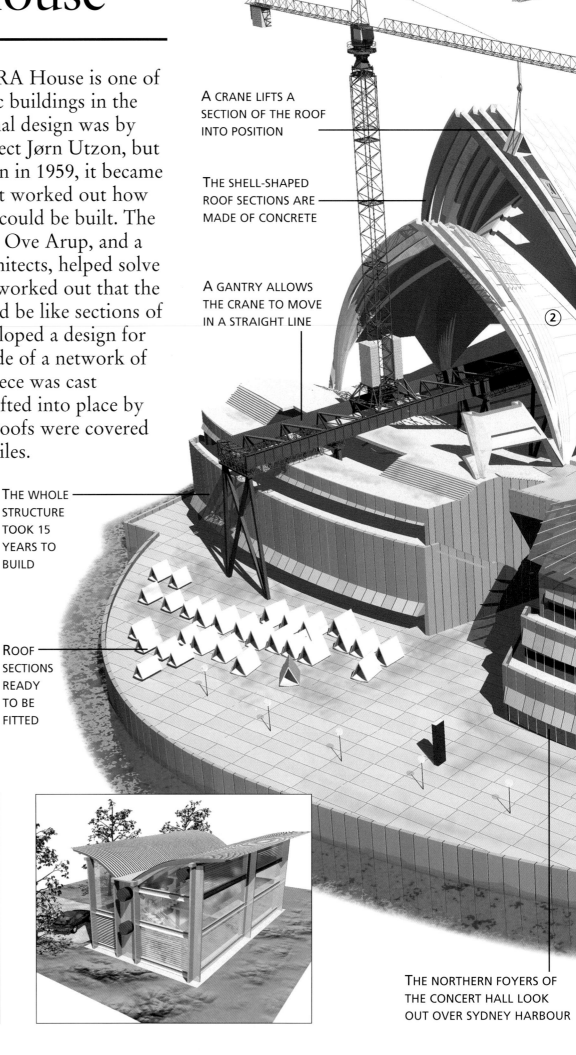

A CRANE LIFTS A SECTION OF THE ROOF INTO POSITION

THE SHELL-SHAPED ROOF SECTIONS ARE MADE OF CONCRETE

A GANTRY ALLOWS THE CRANE TO MOVE IN A STRAIGHT LINE

②

THE WHOLE STRUCTURE TOOK 15 YEARS TO BUILD

ROOF SECTIONS READY TO BE FITTED

THE NORTHERN FOYERS OF THE CONCERT HALL LOOK OUT OVER SYDNEY HARBOUR

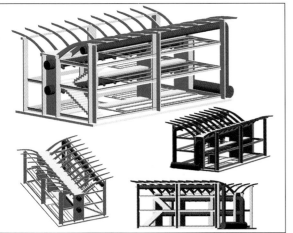

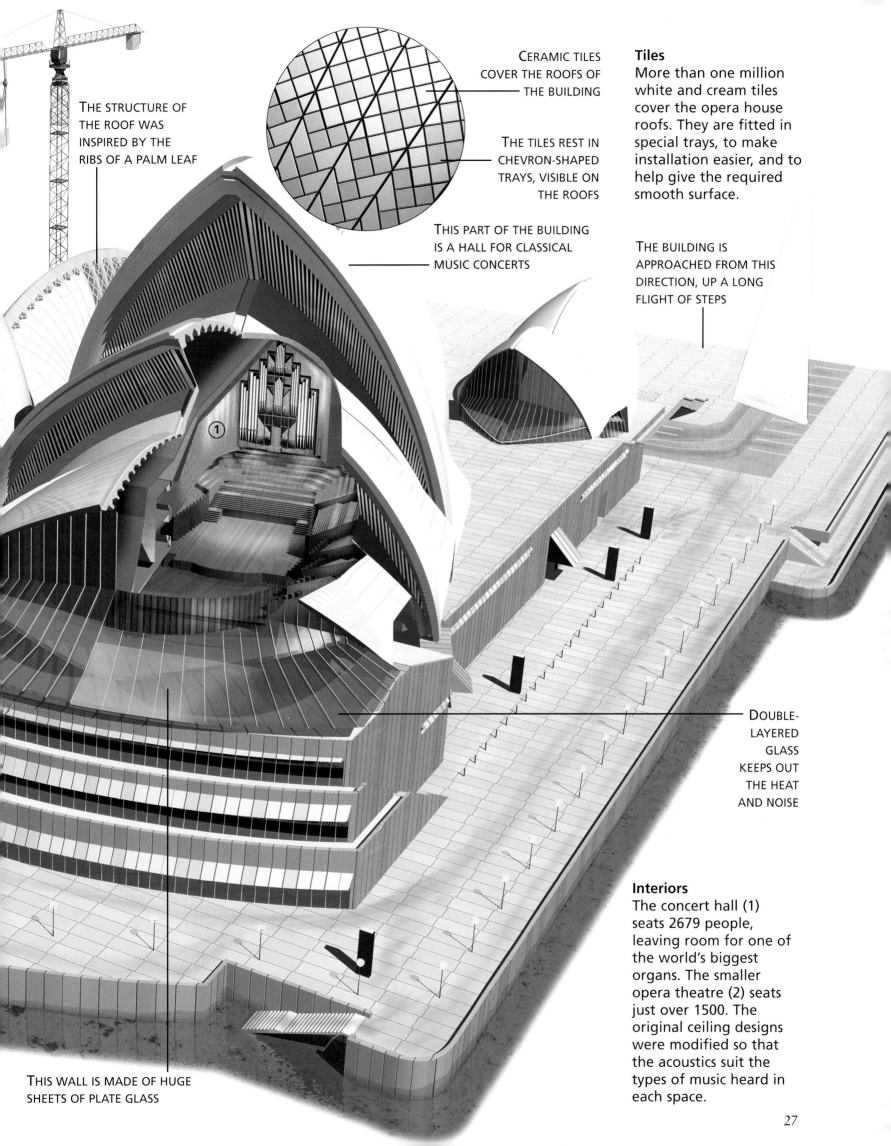

CERAMIC TILES COVER THE ROOFS OF THE BUILDING

THE TILES REST IN CHEVRON-SHAPED TRAYS, VISIBLE ON THE ROOFS

Tiles
More than one million white and cream tiles cover the opera house roofs. They are fitted in special trays, to make installation easier, and to help give the required smooth surface.

THE STRUCTURE OF THE ROOF WAS INSPIRED BY THE RIBS OF A PALM LEAF

THIS PART OF THE BUILDING IS A HALL FOR CLASSICAL MUSIC CONCERTS

THE BUILDING IS APPROACHED FROM THIS DIRECTION, UP A LONG FLIGHT OF STEPS

DOUBLE-LAYERED GLASS KEEPS OUT THE HEAT AND NOISE

THIS WALL IS MADE OF HUGE SHEETS OF PLATE GLASS

Interiors
The concert hall (1) seats 2679 people, leaving room for one of the world's biggest organs. The smaller opera theatre (2) seats just over 1500. The original ceiling designs were modified so that the acoustics suit the types of music heard in each space.

Statue of Liberty

AMERICA'S most famous statue was created in France as a gift from the French people to celebrate the 100th anniversary of American independence. It took about 15 years to build, and was finally unveiled in 1886, 10 years after the anniversary. Ever since, it has stood in New York harbour, reminding visitors and immigrants that they are entering 'the land of the free'. The figure of Liberty was designed by the French sculptor Frédéric-Auguste Bartholdi, put together in Paris, and then taken apart and shipped in more than 200 crates to the USA. The statue is made of a lightweight 'skin' of copper, supported by a strong inner framework. The engineer Gustave Eiffel, creator of the Eiffel Tower in Paris, used his knowledge of bridges and similar structures to design the framework.

Statue and base

By 1883 the French had nearly finished the copper statue, but the Americans were only just starting on the massive base. As well as providing a support for the statue, the base contains stairs, a lift, an outside viewing platform, and a museum. By the time the base was completed, the parts of the statue had been in New York for 15 months. But once the base was finished, work went quickly, with the framework and skin going up in a few months.

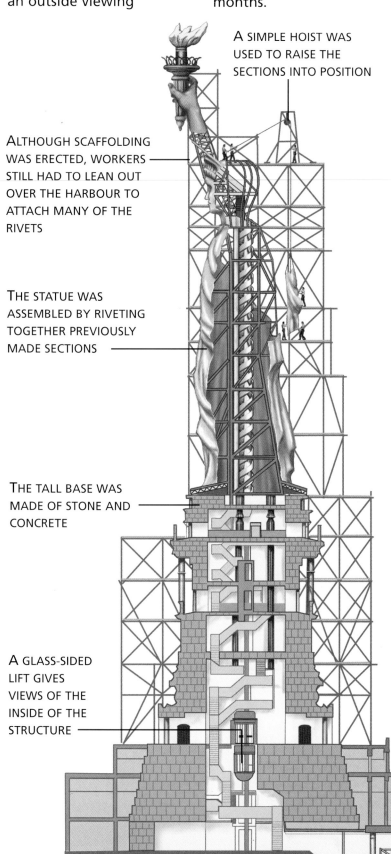

A SIMPLE HOIST WAS USED TO RAISE THE SECTIONS INTO POSITION

ALTHOUGH SCAFFOLDING WAS ERECTED, WORKERS STILL HAD TO LEAN OUT OVER THE HARBOUR TO ATTACH MANY OF THE RIVETS

THE STATUE WAS ASSEMBLED BY RIVETING TOGETHER PREVIOUSLY MADE SECTIONS

THE TALL BASE WAS MADE OF STONE AND CONCRETE

A GLASS-SIDED LIFT GIVES VIEWS OF THE INSIDE OF THE STRUCTURE

Working methods

No statue of this size had been made before, so Bartholdi and his craftsmen had to use special methods. First, a team of model-makers made full-size plaster copies of each part of the statue (*above left*). Then the carpenters got to work, surrounding these plaster body parts with a wooden framework (*above right*). Next, they removed the plaster, to leave a full-size wooden mould. Finally, the metalworkers took sheets of copper, beat them into shape on the insides of the wooden moulds and drilled a series of holes along the edges, so that the sheets could be riveted together.

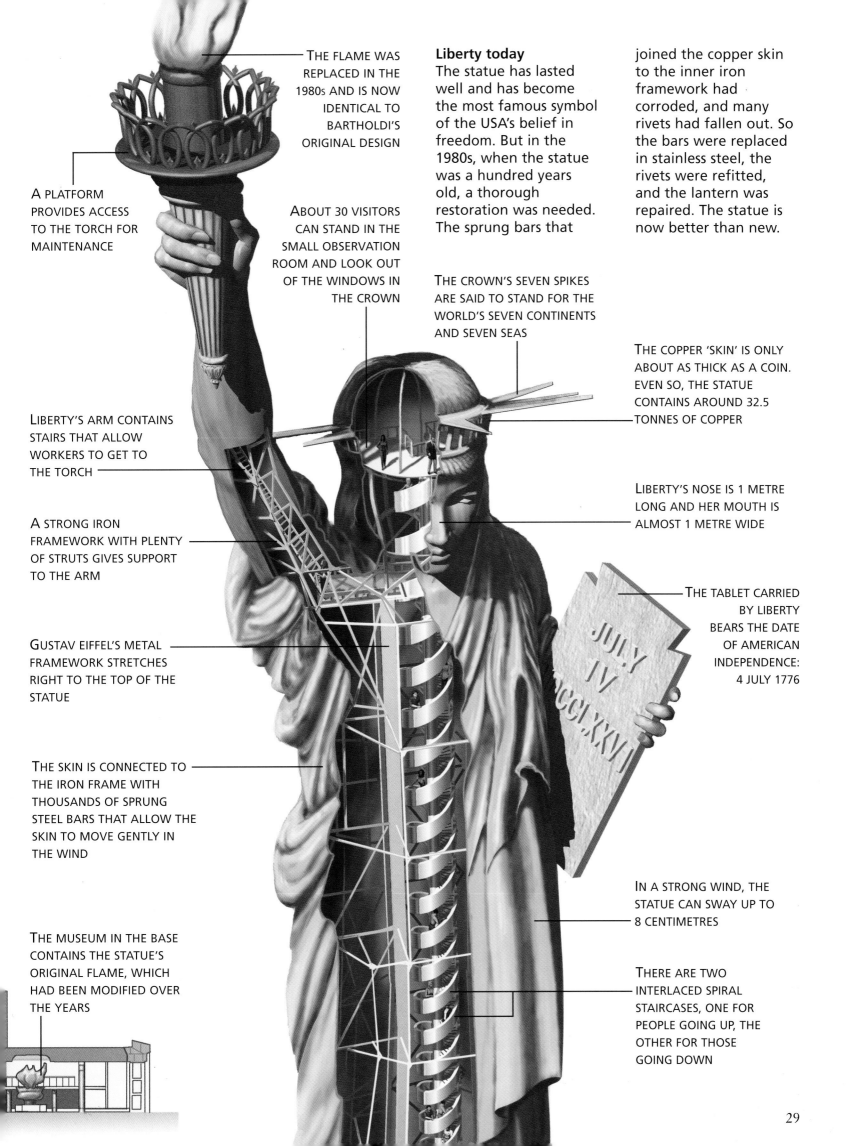

THE FLAME WAS REPLACED IN THE 1980s AND IS NOW IDENTICAL TO BARTHOLDI'S ORIGINAL DESIGN

A PLATFORM PROVIDES ACCESS TO THE TORCH FOR MAINTENANCE

LIBERTY'S ARM CONTAINS STAIRS THAT ALLOW WORKERS TO GET TO THE TORCH

A STRONG IRON FRAMEWORK WITH PLENTY OF STRUTS GIVES SUPPORT TO THE ARM

GUSTAV EIFFEL'S METAL FRAMEWORK STRETCHES RIGHT TO THE TOP OF THE STATUE

THE SKIN IS CONNECTED TO THE IRON FRAME WITH THOUSANDS OF SPRUNG STEEL BARS THAT ALLOW THE SKIN TO MOVE GENTLY IN THE WIND

THE MUSEUM IN THE BASE CONTAINS THE STATUE'S ORIGINAL FLAME, WHICH HAD BEEN MODIFIED OVER THE YEARS

Liberty today

The statue has lasted well and has become the most famous symbol of the USA's belief in freedom. But in the 1980s, when the statue was a hundred years old, a thorough restoration was needed. The sprung bars that joined the copper skin to the inner iron framework had corroded, and many rivets had fallen out. So the bars were replaced in stainless steel, the rivets were refitted, and the lantern was repaired. The statue is now better than new.

ABOUT 30 VISITORS CAN STAND IN THE SMALL OBSERVATION ROOM AND LOOK OUT OF THE WINDOWS IN THE CROWN

THE CROWN'S SEVEN SPIKES ARE SAID TO STAND FOR THE WORLD'S SEVEN CONTINENTS AND SEVEN SEAS

THE COPPER 'SKIN' IS ONLY ABOUT AS THICK AS A COIN. EVEN SO, THE STATUE CONTAINS AROUND 32.5 TONNES OF COPPER

LIBERTY'S NOSE IS 1 METRE LONG AND HER MOUTH IS ALMOST 1 METRE WIDE

THE TABLET CARRIED BY LIBERTY BEARS THE DATE OF AMERICAN INDEPENDENCE: 4 JULY 1776

JULY IV MDCCLXXVI

IN A STRONG WIND, THE STATUE CAN SWAY UP TO 8 CENTIMETRES

THERE ARE TWO INTERLACED SPIRAL STAIRCASES, ONE FOR PEOPLE GOING UP, THE OTHER FOR THOSE GOING DOWN

Bridges

TODAY'S engineers are always looking for better ways of building bridges over long spans (distances). In the 19th and early 20th centuries they often built suspension bridges. Today, cable-stayed bridges are more popular because they are not too expensive to build and because they do not need the huge anchorage points required by suspension bridges. In a cable-stayed bridge, long metal cables join the roadway to one or more tall pylons (towers), and so transfer the structure's weight to its foundations. One of the most beautiful cable-stayed bridges is the Pont de Normandie (*right*), which spans the River Seine in northern France. After it had opened in the 1990s journey routes and times were dramatically shortened between Normandy and the Channel ports of Boulogne and Calais.

Supporting pylons
The cables are anchored to two concrete pylons, each of which is 200 metres tall. Shaped like an upside-down letter Y, each pylon is designed to be stable and to offer low resistance to the wind.

STEEL IS USED FOR THE CABLES BECAUSE IT IS STRONG, EVEN WHEN STRETCHED

AS THE BRIDGE WAS BUILT, MORE CABLES WERE LINKED TO THESE ANCHOR POINTS

THE PONT DE NORMANDIE IS 2141 METRES LONG

THE PILES PASS THROUGH CLAY AND INTO LIMESTONE

APPROACH SPANS (THE OUTER SECTIONS) HAVE A CONCRETE DECK, BUILT TO THE SAME SHAPE AS THE CENTRAL DECK

PILES ARE SUNK DEEP INTO THE BANKS OF THE RIVER TO SUPPORT CONCRETE PIERS, ON WHICH THE APPROACH SPANS ARE BUILT

PILES, DRIVEN THROUGH THE SOIL TO THE BEDROCK BELOW, PROVIDE A SECURE BASE FOR THE TALL PYLONS

A CONCRETE BARRIER CALLED A COFFERDAM PROTECTS THE BASE OF THE PYLON FROM PASSING SHIPS

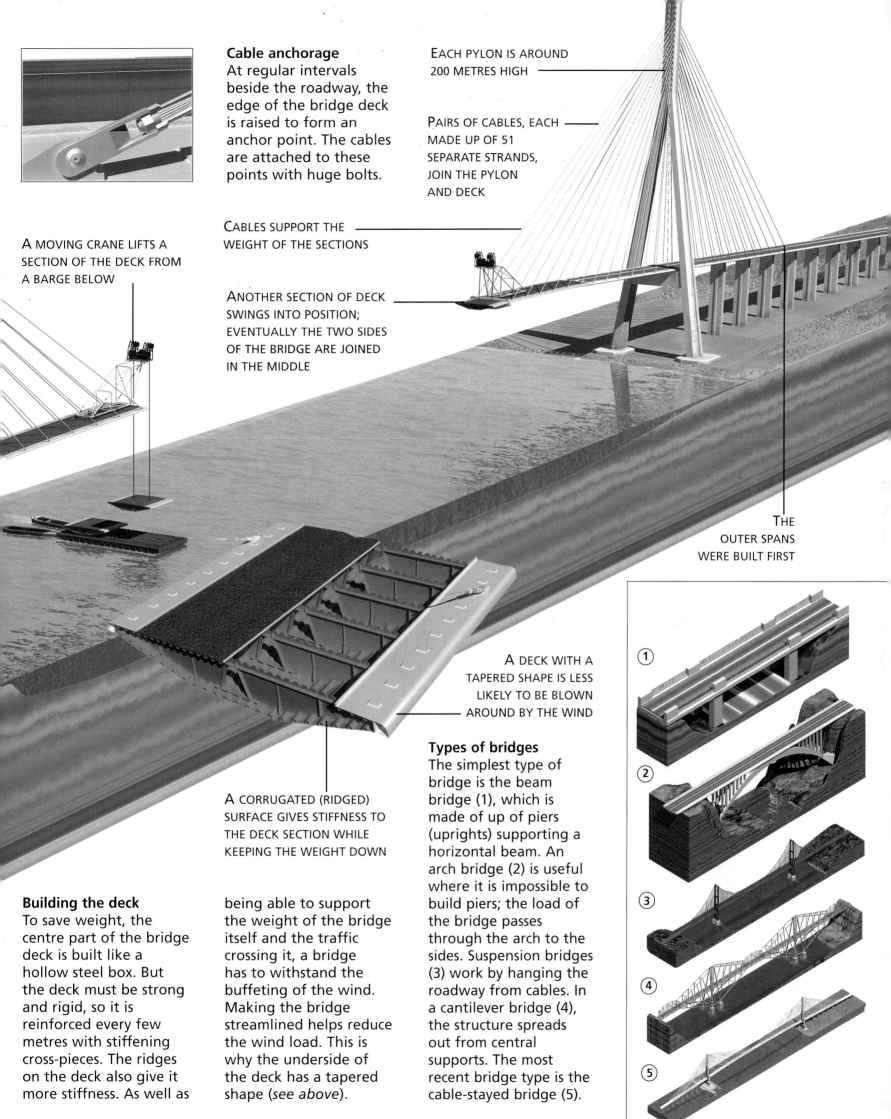

Cable anchorage
At regular intervals beside the roadway, the edge of the bridge deck is raised to form an anchor point. The cables are attached to these points with huge bolts.

EACH PYLON IS AROUND 200 METRES HIGH

PAIRS OF CABLES, EACH MADE UP OF 51 SEPARATE STRANDS, JOIN THE PYLON AND DECK

CABLES SUPPORT THE WEIGHT OF THE SECTIONS

A MOVING CRANE LIFTS A SECTION OF THE DECK FROM A BARGE BELOW

ANOTHER SECTION OF DECK SWINGS INTO POSITION; EVENTUALLY THE TWO SIDES OF THE BRIDGE ARE JOINED IN THE MIDDLE

THE OUTER SPANS WERE BUILT FIRST

A DECK WITH A TAPERED SHAPE IS LESS LIKELY TO BE BLOWN AROUND BY THE WIND

A CORRUGATED (RIDGED) SURFACE GIVES STIFFNESS TO THE DECK SECTION WHILE KEEPING THE WEIGHT DOWN

Building the deck
To save weight, the centre part of the bridge deck is built like a hollow steel box. But the deck must be strong and rigid, so it is reinforced every few metres with stiffening cross-pieces. The ridges on the deck also give it more stiffness. As well as being able to support the weight of the bridge itself and the traffic crossing it, a bridge has to withstand the buffeting of the wind. Making the bridge streamlined helps reduce the wind load. This is why the underside of the deck has a tapered shape (*see above*).

Types of bridges
The simplest type of bridge is the beam bridge (1), which is made of up of piers (uprights) supporting a horizontal beam. An arch bridge (2) is useful where it is impossible to build piers; the load of the bridge passes through the arch to the sides. Suspension bridges (3) work by hanging the roadway from cables. In a cantilever bridge (4), the structure spreads out from central supports. The most recent bridge type is the cable-stayed bridge (5).

① ② ③ ④ ⑤

Channel Tunnel

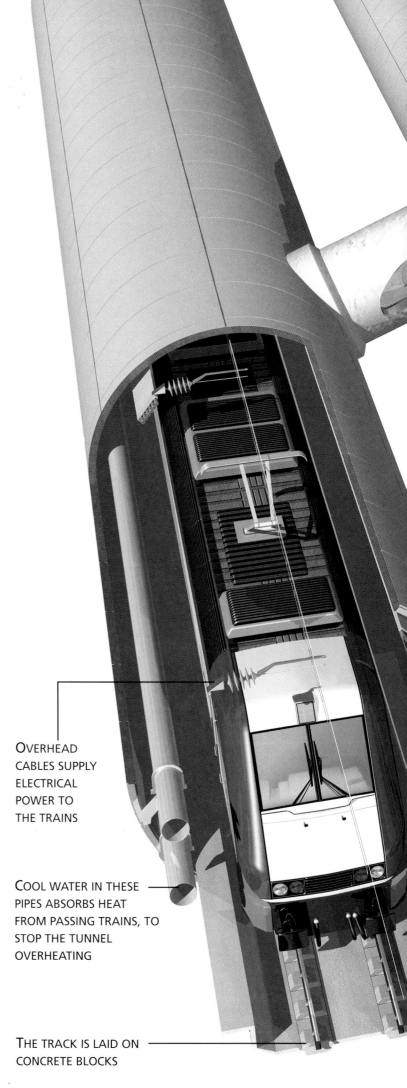

THE TUNNEL that connects England and France was a massive engineering project. Builders had to remove around 7 million cubic metres of rock, install some 200 kilometres of railway track, and fit more than 1300 kilometres of wiring. As a result, train passengers can now travel from Paris to London in around three hours. Car users can drive on to one of the special shuttle trains and cross from one country to the other in 30 minutes. Engineers had to build huge tunnel-boring machines to cut through the rock and remove the waste material. They had to create the strongest concrete ever produced for the tunnel linings, and design systems to protect the trains from fire damage. They also had to find a way of reducing the build-up of air pressure that occurs when trains speed through tunnels.

OVERHEAD CABLES SUPPLY ELECTRICAL POWER TO THE TRAINS

COOL WATER IN THESE PIPES ABSORBS HEAT FROM PASSING TRAINS, TO STOP THE TUNNEL OVERHEATING

THE TRACK IS LAID ON CONCRETE BLOCKS

Cutting machines
The tunnels were bored with some of the most massive machines ever constructed. Each tunnel-boring machine had an 800-tonne cutting head faced with rows of picks made of tough tungsten carbide metal. As the cutting head turned, the picks gouged away the rock, which was pushed back through the machine to waiting trains behind.

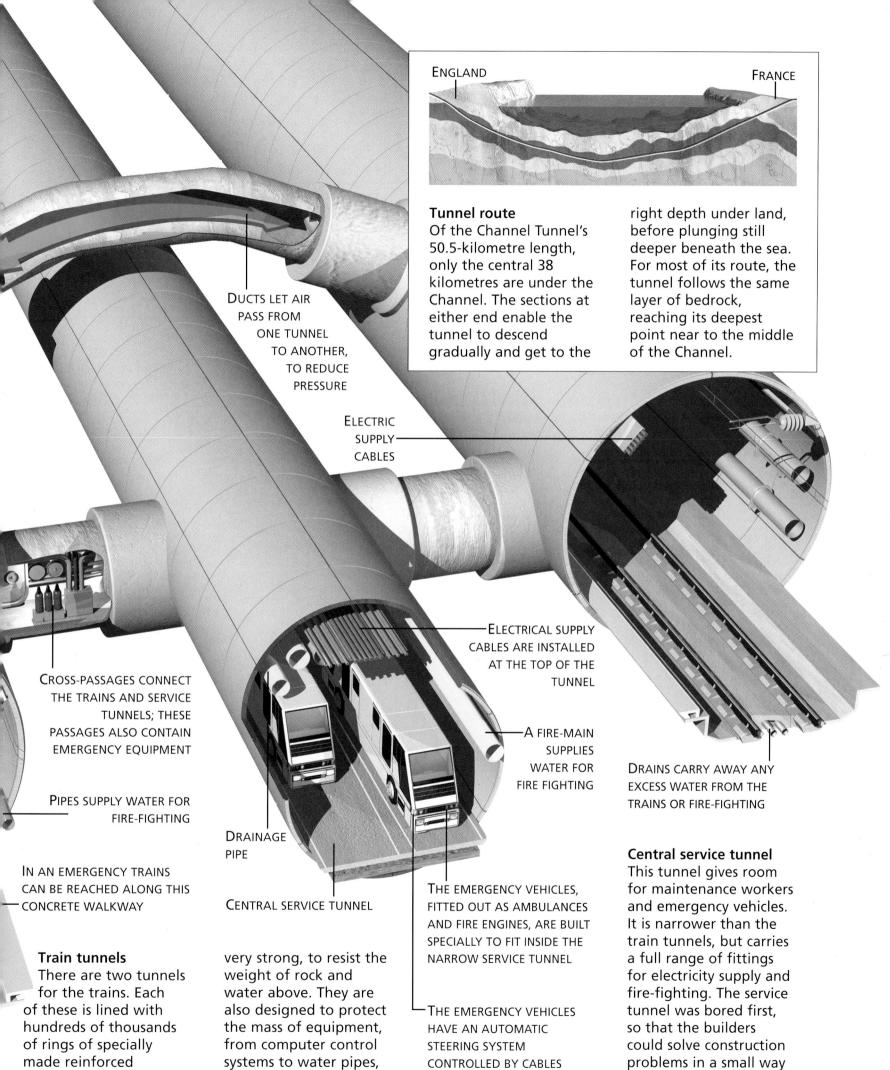

DUCTS LET AIR PASS FROM ONE TUNNEL TO ANOTHER, TO REDUCE PRESSURE

ELECTRIC SUPPLY CABLES

Tunnel route
Of the Channel Tunnel's 50.5-kilometre length, only the central 38 kilometres are under the Channel. The sections at either end enable the tunnel to descend gradually and get to the right depth under land, before plunging still deeper beneath the sea. For most of its route, the tunnel follows the same layer of bedrock, reaching its deepest point near to the middle of the Channel.

ELECTRICAL SUPPLY CABLES ARE INSTALLED AT THE TOP OF THE TUNNEL

CROSS-PASSAGES CONNECT THE TRAINS AND SERVICE TUNNELS; THESE PASSAGES ALSO CONTAIN EMERGENCY EQUIPMENT

A FIRE-MAIN SUPPLIES WATER FOR FIRE FIGHTING

DRAINS CARRY AWAY ANY EXCESS WATER FROM THE TRAINS OR FIRE-FIGHTING

PIPES SUPPLY WATER FOR FIRE-FIGHTING

IN AN EMERGENCY TRAINS CAN BE REACHED ALONG THIS CONCRETE WALKWAY

DRAINAGE PIPE

CENTRAL SERVICE TUNNEL

THE EMERGENCY VEHICLES, FITTED OUT AS AMBULANCES AND FIRE ENGINES, ARE BUILT SPECIALLY TO FIT INSIDE THE NARROW SERVICE TUNNEL

Central service tunnel
This tunnel gives room for maintenance workers and emergency vehicles. It is narrower than the train tunnels, but carries a full range of fittings for electricity supply and fire-fighting. The service tunnel was bored first, so that the builders could solve construction problems in a small way before starting on the larger tunnels.

Train tunnels
There are two tunnels for the trains. Each of these is lined with hundreds of thousands of rings of specially made reinforced concrete. The tunnel walls are designed to be very strong, to resist the weight of rock and water above. They are also designed to protect the mass of equipment, from computer control systems to water pipes, that the tunnel also contains.

THE EMERGENCY VEHICLES HAVE AN AUTOMATIC STEERING SYSTEM CONTROLLED BY CABLES UNDER THE ROADWAY

Airport

WHEN THE Japanese authorities needed a new international airport in the 1990s, they built one of the most unusual buildings ever. Kansai Airport, which opened in 1994, is on a specially made artificial island about 5 kilometres away from Japan's main island, Honshu. Because the airport is away from cities, noisy aircraft can land and take off all the time, even at night. Another unusual feature is the terminal building, designed by Italian architect Renzo Piano. Like many modern buildings, it is made mainly of steel and glass. These materials allow quick, easy construction, and can make buildings with spacious floors and lots of sunlight. At Kansai, steel is used to give another advantage. Japan is in a major earthquake zone, so the whole structure is built so that it will withstand earth movements.

Y-SHAPED BRIDGES EACH ACCOMMODATE TWO AIRCRAFT

THE TERMINAL IS 1.6 KILOMETRES LONG AND HAS 41 PLACES FOR AIRCRAFT TO PARK

KANSAI AIRPORT HAS A SINGLE RUNWAY

TO CREATE THE ISLAND A MASSIVE SEA WALL WAS BUILT AROUND THE SITE, THEN THE AREA IN THE MIDDLE WAS FILLED IN

A SEA WALL PROTECTS THE ISLAND

THE EFFECTS OF NOISE AND POLLUTION WERE REDUCED BY PUTTING THE AIRPORT ON AN ISLAND

RAILWAY LINES LIE UNDER THE ROADWAY

Access bridge
Passengers reach the airport by crossing Osaka Bay on a long, two-storey bridge connected to one corner of the island.

THE ISLAND IS JOINED TO THE MAINLAND BY BOTH ROAD AND RAIL LINKS

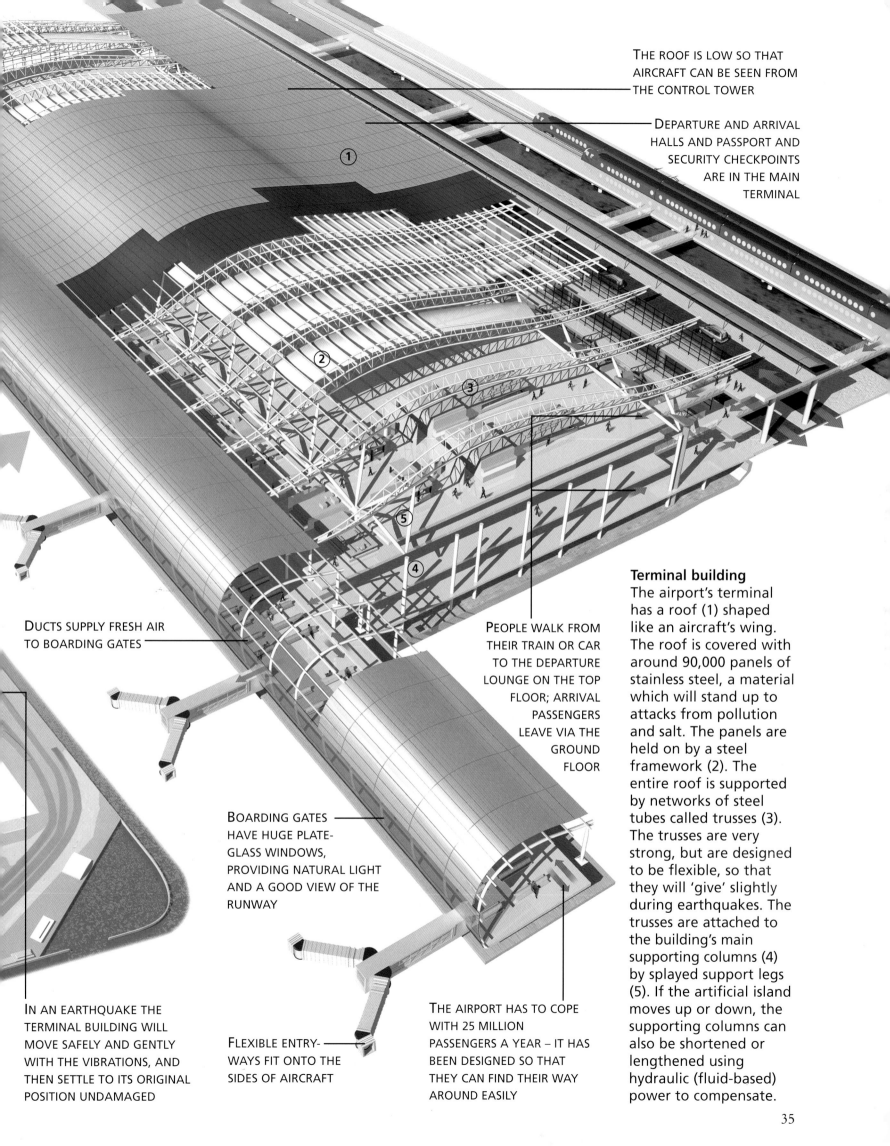

THE ROOF IS LOW SO THAT AIRCRAFT CAN BE SEEN FROM THE CONTROL TOWER

DEPARTURE AND ARRIVAL HALLS AND PASSPORT AND SECURITY CHECKPOINTS ARE IN THE MAIN TERMINAL

① ② ③ ⑤ ④

DUCTS SUPPLY FRESH AIR TO BOARDING GATES

PEOPLE WALK FROM THEIR TRAIN OR CAR TO THE DEPARTURE LOUNGE ON THE TOP FLOOR; ARRIVAL PASSENGERS LEAVE VIA THE GROUND FLOOR

BOARDING GATES HAVE HUGE PLATE-GLASS WINDOWS, PROVIDING NATURAL LIGHT AND A GOOD VIEW OF THE RUNWAY

IN AN EARTHQUAKE THE TERMINAL BUILDING WILL MOVE SAFELY AND GENTLY WITH THE VIBRATIONS, AND THEN SETTLE TO ITS ORIGINAL POSITION UNDAMAGED

FLEXIBLE ENTRY-WAYS FIT ONTO THE SIDES OF AIRCRAFT

THE AIRPORT HAS TO COPE WITH 25 MILLION PASSENGERS A YEAR – IT HAS BEEN DESIGNED SO THAT THEY CAN FIND THEIR WAY AROUND EASILY

Terminal building
The airport's terminal has a roof (1) shaped like an aircraft's wing. The roof is covered with around 90,000 panels of stainless steel, a material which will stand up to attacks from pollution and salt. The panels are held on by a steel framework (2). The entire roof is supported by networks of steel tubes called trusses (3). The trusses are very strong, but are designed to be flexible, so that they will 'give' slightly during earthquakes. The trusses are attached to the building's main supporting columns (4) by splayed support legs (5). If the artificial island moves up or down, the supporting columns can also be shortened or lengthened using hydraulic (fluid-based) power to compensate.

Ports and Docks

ALL OVER the world, ports provide a safe place for ships to moor, load, and unload. If there is not too much difference between the water levels at high and low tides, the port can be open to the sea. If there is a big variation in the tides, the port has to be closed off from the open sea, and ships must reach it through the twin gates of a sea lock. Building this type of port can be a major construction project. Piles need to be driven deep into the ground to make a waterproof harbour wall. Special quays and wharves, designed to accommodate today's large cargo ships, need to be constructed. The tide continuously washes sand into the port and erodes away the walls, so the harbour authorities have to work hard to maintain the port by dredging the harbour bottom to keep the correct depth of water and by building up the protective outer wall.

Port traffic
All sorts of specialized ships can be seen around a modern port. Many of these, like oil tankers (1), bulk grain carriers (2), and other cargo vessels (3), are loading and unloading. Others (4) have come to the port to be mended or refitted in the dry dock. There are also ships that help in the maintenance of the port itself. Many of these are dredgers, such as the hopper dredger (5) and scoop dredger (6), which remove sand and rocks that build up on the harbour bed.

RAILWAY SIDINGS TAKE FREIGHT TRAINS ALONGSIDE IMPORTANT WAREHOUSES

BULK GRAIN CARRIERS ARE LOADED DIRECTLY FROM A GRAIN STORE

A ROAD LINK TO AN OIL TERMINAL AND LIGHTHOUSE

A LIGHTHOUSE FLASHES A WARNING TO PASSING SHIPS

Lock gates
When a ship leaves port, one set of lock gates is opened and the vessel sails into the lock (see above, *upper left*). Next these gates are closed, and water is drained out of the lock until the level inside is the same as the current sea level. Then the other gates are opened and the ship can sail out (*lower right*).

A BARGE WITH A CRANE LAYS ROCKS TO PROTECT THE HARBOUR WALL

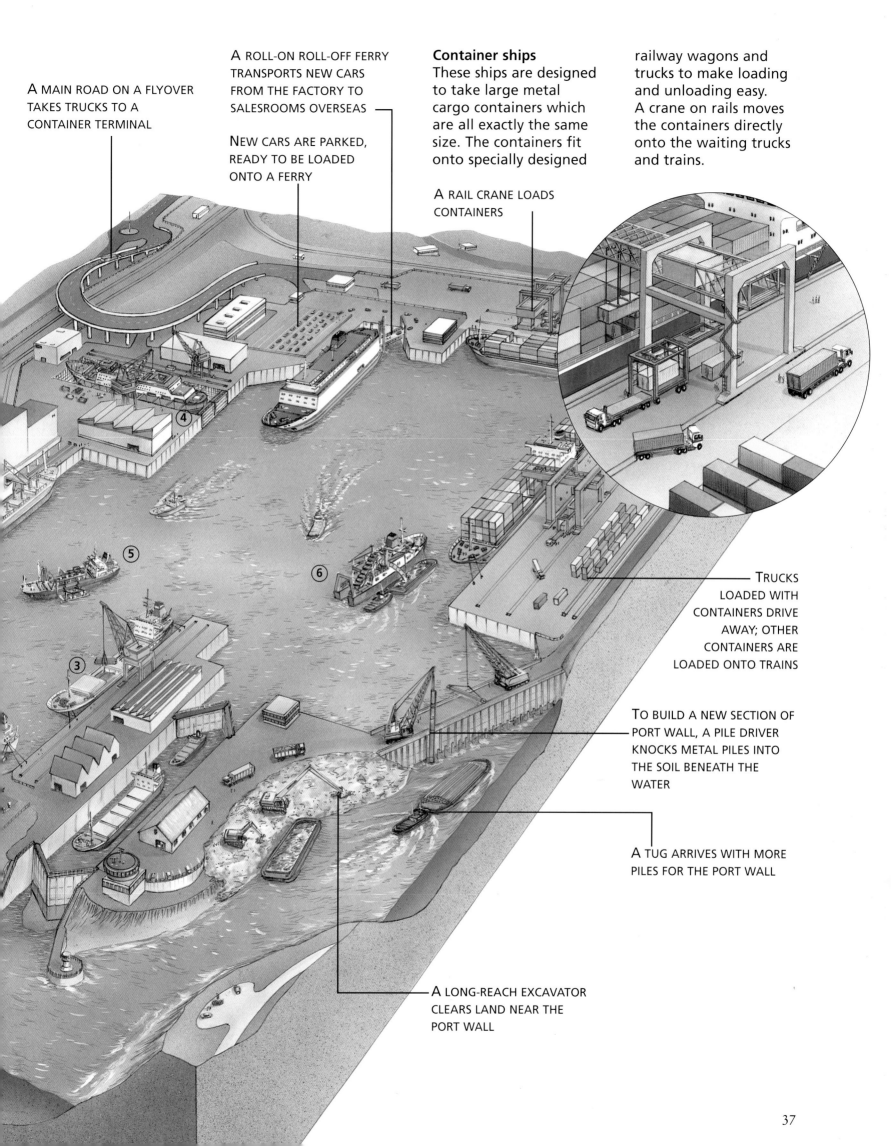

A MAIN ROAD ON A FLYOVER TAKES TRUCKS TO A CONTAINER TERMINAL

A ROLL-ON ROLL-OFF FERRY TRANSPORTS NEW CARS FROM THE FACTORY TO SALESROOMS OVERSEAS

NEW CARS ARE PARKED, READY TO BE LOADED ONTO A FERRY

Container ships
These ships are designed to take large metal cargo containers which are all exactly the same size. The containers fit onto specially designed railway wagons and trucks to make loading and unloading easy. A crane on rails moves the containers directly onto the waiting trucks and trains.

A RAIL CRANE LOADS CONTAINERS

TRUCKS LOADED WITH CONTAINERS DRIVE AWAY; OTHER CONTAINERS ARE LOADED ONTO TRAINS

TO BUILD A NEW SECTION OF PORT WALL, A PILE DRIVER KNOCKS METAL PILES INTO THE SOIL BENEATH THE WATER

A TUG ARRIVES WITH MORE PILES FOR THE PORT WALL

A LONG-REACH EXCAVATOR CLEARS LAND NEAR THE PORT WALL

Oil Rigs

TO FIND oil, engineers often have to use an oil rig to drill into rock deep under the sea bed. Oil rigs are some of the most massive structures ever built. Some stand on huge concrete legs that reach from the sea bed to the surface of the water, and are topped with vast super-structures (upper areas) with room for many people and heavy machines. A rig is as high as a skyscraper, so tall tower cranes are needed to build it. It has to be big enough to house hundreds of workers, together with their laboratories, control rooms, offices, and stores. In addition, rigs need pumping machinery, equipment to separate oil from the natural gas found with it, and a drill housed in a derrick, a tall structure the height of an apartment building.

Drill string and derrick
A long pipe, called the drill string, is joined to the drill bit (tip) and runs up through the rig. It is supported by the derrick, the pylon-like metal tower at the top of the rig. At the foot of the derrick is the mechanism that turns the drill string.

THE DERRICK

WORKSHOPS AND CONTROL ROOMS

A BALCONY CONTAINS LIFE-BOATS AND RESCUE EQUIPMENT

THIS LEG CONTAINS RISER PIPES THAT BRING UP OIL DIRECTLY FROM THE WELLS BELOW

ONE OF FOUR MAIN LEGS THAT SUPPORT THE WEIGHT OF THE TOP SECTION OF THE RIG

BALLAST TANKS PUSH THE RIG DOWN AND KEEP IT STABLE

SOME OF THE RIG'S TANKS ARE USED FOR OIL STORAGE

AS THE BALLAST TANKS ARE FILLED, THE OIL RIG SINKS DOWN INTO POSITION

THE DRILL BIT MUST REACH OIL DEEP UNDER THE SEA BED

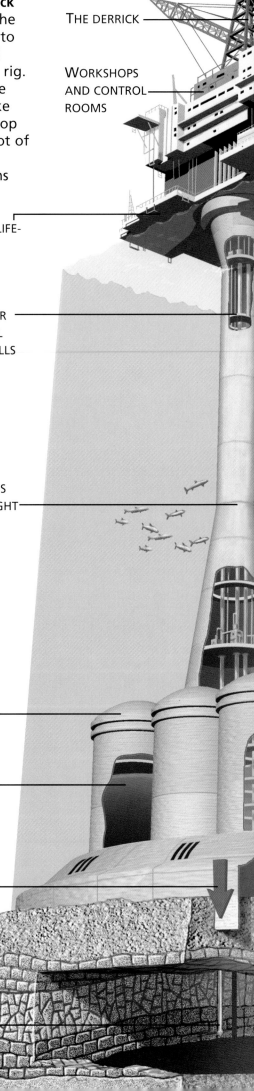

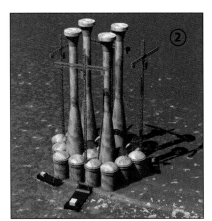

Rig construction
This rig was built from the base up, starting with the large ballast tanks (1). Tower cranes were used to construct the main legs (2) and add the superstructure. Because of its empty tanks the structure could float and was towed out to sea by a small fleet of tugs (3). The tanks were then filled, forcing it to sink.

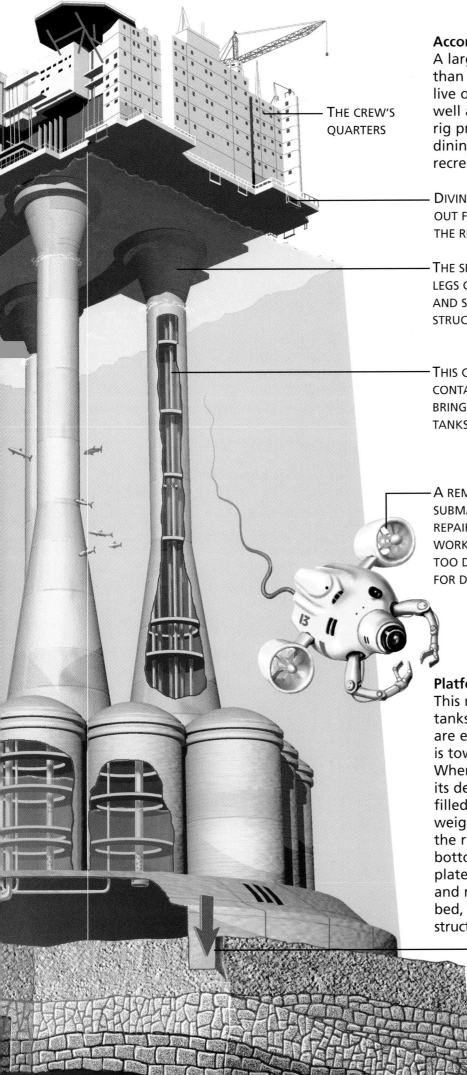

Accommodation

A large rig needs more than 200 workers, who live on the platform. As well as their rooms, the rig provides kitchens, a dining room, and recreation rooms.

THE CREW'S QUARTERS

DIVING PLATFORMS STICK OUT FROM THE SIDE OF THE RIG

THE SPLAYED TOPS TO THE LEGS GIVE EXTRA STRENGTH AND STIFFNESS TO THE STRUCTURE

THIS CONCRETE LEG CONTAINS PIPES WHICH BRING UP OIL FROM THE TANKS BELOW

A REMOTE-OPERATED MINI-SUBMARINE IS USED FOR REPAIR AND MAINTENANCE WORK IN WATERS THAT ARE TOO DEEP OR DANGEROUS FOR DIVERS

Platform base

This rig has huge ballast tanks at the base. These are empty when the rig is towed out to sea. When the rig arrives at its destination, they are filled with water to weigh the rig down. As the rig rests on the sea bottom, heavy anchor plates dig into the sand and rocks on the sea bed, to make the vast structure still more stable.

ANCHOR PLATES PREVENT THE RIG FROM DRIFTING

Types of rig

On a fixed rig (1) the legs are sunk straight into the sea bed; this type of rig is therefore best in shallow seas. A jack-up rig (2), suitable for water up to 100 metres deep, is raised up on larger legs. For still deeper seas, a floating rig (3) is used. This type of rig is kept still by vast ballast tanks and numerous anchors on the sea bottom.

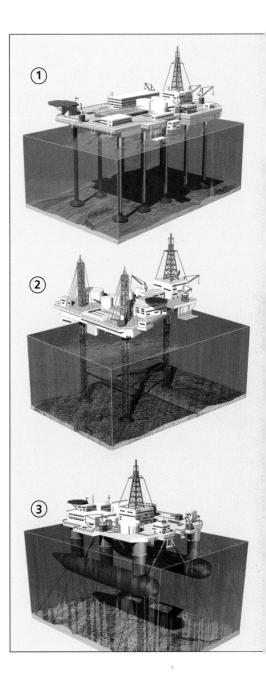

OIL DEPOSITS LIE DEEP UNDER THE SEA BED

Dams

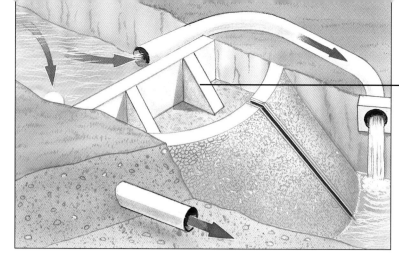

THE HEAVIEST structures made by people are dams. They contain millions of tonnes of earth, rock, or concrete. Today, most dams are designed to produce electricity by harnessing the power of rushing water. One of the most famous modern dams is the Itaipú Dam across the River Paraná, on the border of Brazil and Paraguay. It took 10 years to build and rises almost 200 metres above the river bed. It is a complicated structure, made up of several linked dams. Part of the dam is made of hollow concrete segments, another part is earth-filled, and a third section is filled with rock with strong outer supports of concrete. The dam shown here is based on the rock-filled section of Itaipú.

Cofferdam

Before constructing a dam, the engineers usually have to build a temporary dam, called a cofferdam, to keep the water away. First, they divert the river into a separate channel, then they construct the cofferdam. Water that builds up behind the cofferdam can then be piped to a point downriver of the main dam.

EACH REINFORCED CONCRETE POWERHOUSE CONTAINS A TOTAL OF TEN TURBINES AND GENERATORS, EACH SUPPLIED WITH WATER BY ITS OWN PENSTOCK

HEAVY SLOPING SUPPORTS, CALLED BUTTRESSES, STRENGTHEN THE DAM

THE WALL OF A DAM HOLDS BACK WATER TO FORM A RESERVOIR BEHIND

OVERHEAD CABLES CARRY ELECTRICITY AWAY FROM THE DAM

THE MAIN SPILLWAY – IF THE WATER-LEVEL IN THE RESERVOIR RISES TOO HIGH, WATER IS RELEASED DOWN THE SPILLWAY

POWER HOUSES CONTAINING MORE GENERATORS

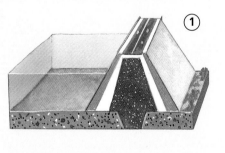
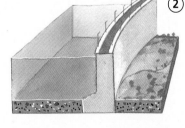
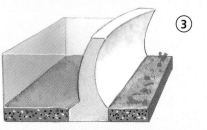
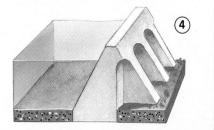

WATER EMERGES FROM THE BASE OF THE TURBINE

Different dams

Earthfill dams (1) are made of a core of compressed clay, plus layers of earth and stone. Arch dams (2) are built in narrow gorges. Their curve points into the current, so that the water pushes the dam into the sides of the gorge. A cupola dam (3) has a double curve, giving its thin walls extra strength, like an eggshell. A gravity dam (4), uses its weight to hold back the water. The Itaipú Dam is a combination of types 1, 2, and 4.

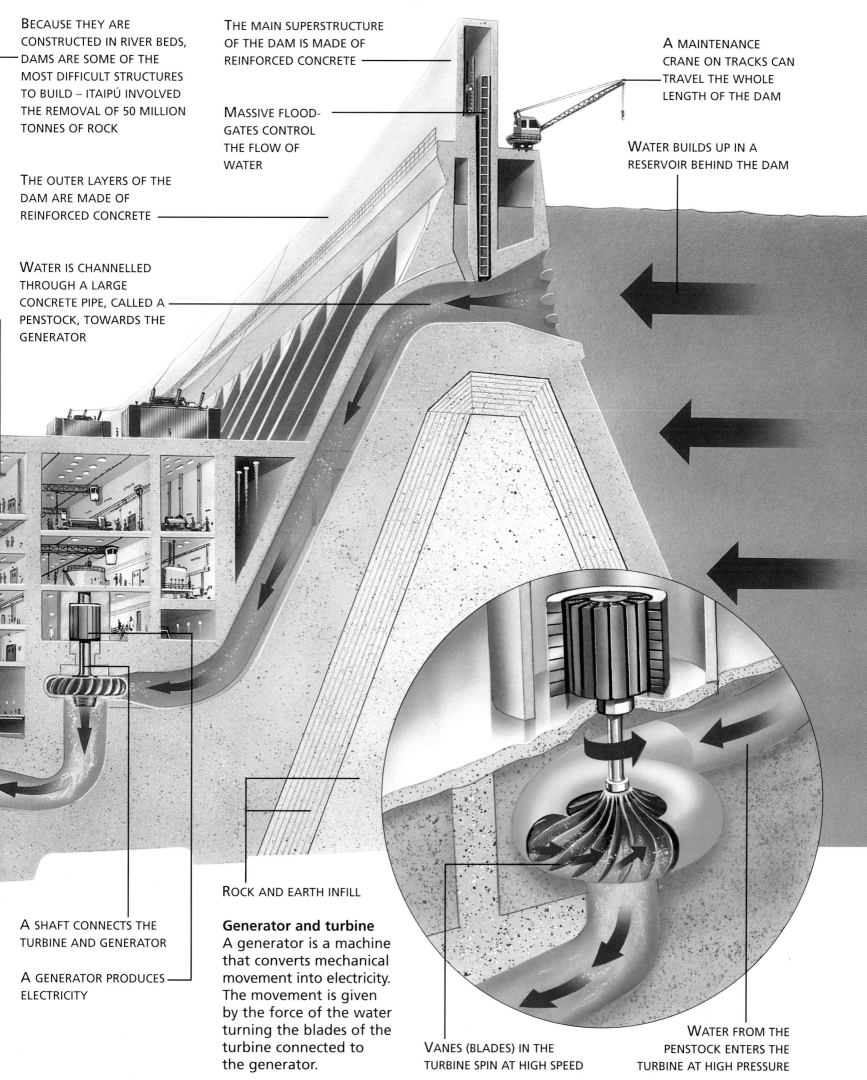

BECAUSE THEY ARE CONSTRUCTED IN RIVER BEDS, DAMS ARE SOME OF THE MOST DIFFICULT STRUCTURES TO BUILD – ITAIPÚ INVOLVED THE REMOVAL OF 50 MILLION TONNES OF ROCK

THE MAIN SUPERSTRUCTURE OF THE DAM IS MADE OF REINFORCED CONCRETE

A MAINTENANCE CRANE ON TRACKS CAN TRAVEL THE WHOLE LENGTH OF THE DAM

MASSIVE FLOOD-GATES CONTROL THE FLOW OF WATER

WATER BUILDS UP IN A RESERVOIR BEHIND THE DAM

THE OUTER LAYERS OF THE DAM ARE MADE OF REINFORCED CONCRETE

WATER IS CHANNELLED THROUGH A LARGE CONCRETE PIPE, CALLED A PENSTOCK, TOWARDS THE GENERATOR

ROCK AND EARTH INFILL

A SHAFT CONNECTS THE TURBINE AND GENERATOR

A GENERATOR PRODUCES ELECTRICITY

Generator and turbine
A generator is a machine that converts mechanical movement into electricity. The movement is given by the force of the water turning the blades of the turbine connected to the generator.

VANES (BLADES) IN THE TURBINE SPIN AT HIGH SPEED

WATER FROM THE PENSTOCK ENTERS THE TURBINE AT HIGH PRESSURE

Growth of a City

MANY CITIES began, like New York, with a few houses next to a natural harbour. Soon a road system was built, providing routes through the town and links to other places. In the 19th century, industry developed, and with it the need for better transport. People found ways of fitting railways into crowded city centres – often by building them underground. New sources of power were discovered, too. Gas and electricity began to light 19th-century city streets, and people wanted these services in their homes, too. So the streets were dug up to lay pipes and wires and to build sewers to remove waste. Meanwhile, cities were growing outwards and upwards as populations grew. They had become the bustling, exciting places that they are today.

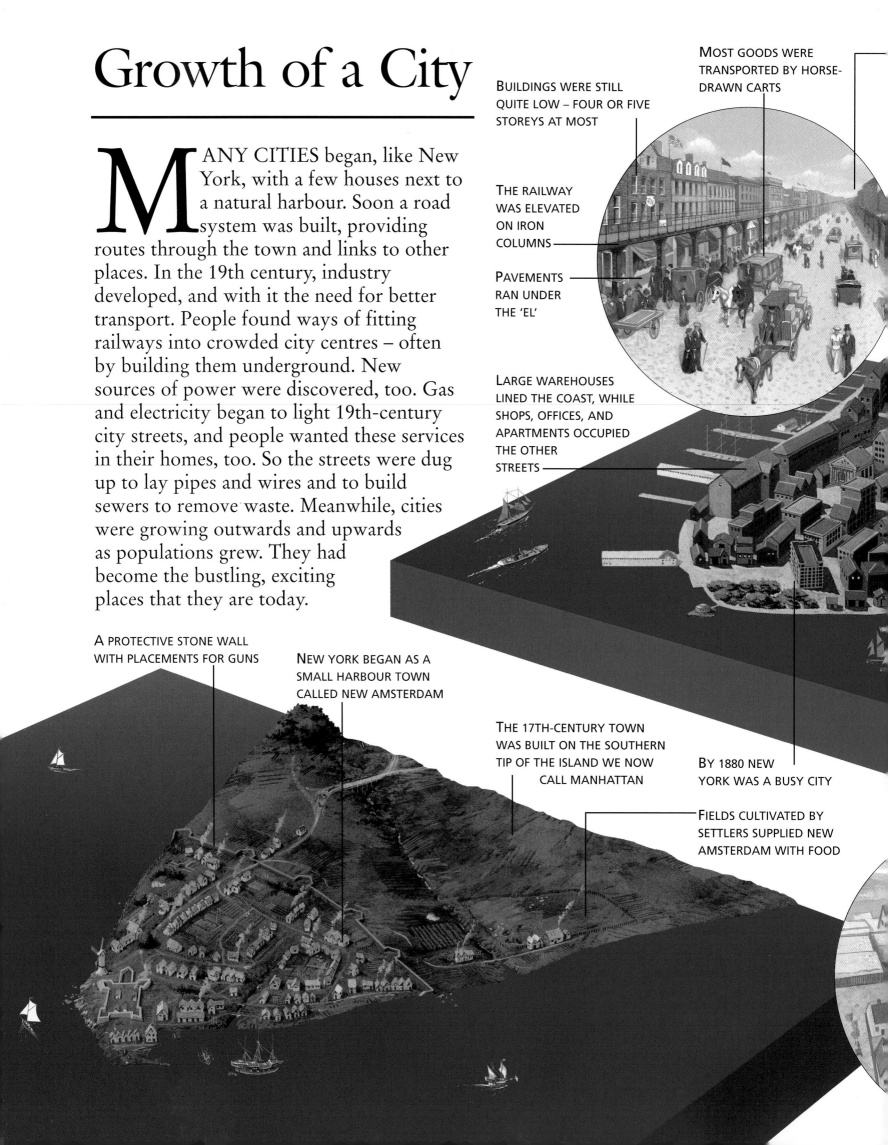

MOST GOODS WERE TRANSPORTED BY HORSE-DRAWN CARTS

BUILDINGS WERE STILL QUITE LOW – FOUR OR FIVE STOREYS AT MOST

THE RAILWAY WAS ELEVATED ON IRON COLUMNS

PAVEMENTS RAN UNDER THE 'EL'

LARGE WAREHOUSES LINED THE COAST, WHILE SHOPS, OFFICES, AND APARTMENTS OCCUPIED THE OTHER STREETS

A PROTECTIVE STONE WALL WITH PLACEMENTS FOR GUNS

NEW YORK BEGAN AS A SMALL HARBOUR TOWN CALLED NEW AMSTERDAM

THE 17TH-CENTURY TOWN WAS BUILT ON THE SOUTHERN TIP OF THE ISLAND WE NOW CALL MANHATTAN

BY 1880 NEW YORK WAS A BUSY CITY

FIELDS CULTIVATED BY SETTLERS SUPPLIED NEW AMSTERDAM WITH FOOD

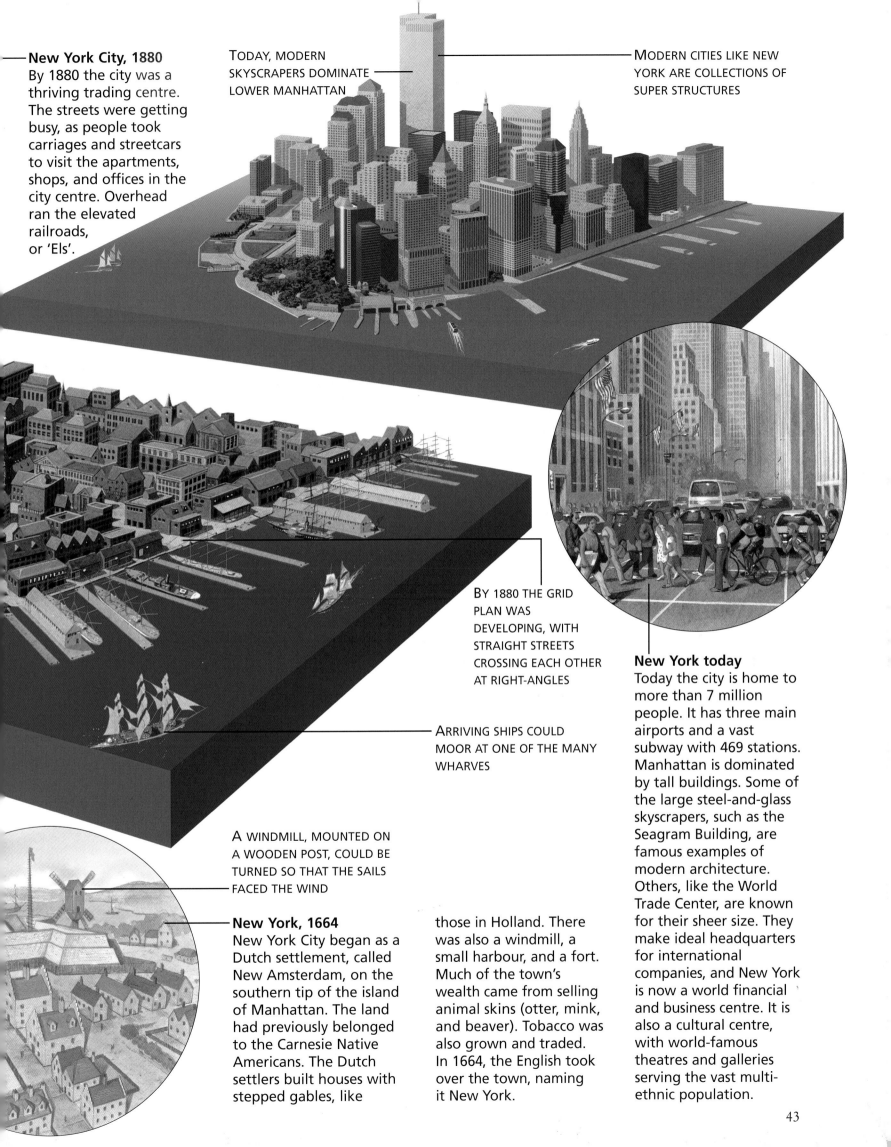

New York City, 1880
By 1880 the city was a thriving trading centre. The streets were getting busy, as people took carriages and streetcars to visit the apartments, shops, and offices in the city centre. Overhead ran the elevated railroads, or 'Els'.

TODAY, MODERN SKYSCRAPERS DOMINATE LOWER MANHATTAN

MODERN CITIES LIKE NEW YORK ARE COLLECTIONS OF SUPER STRUCTURES

BY 1880 THE GRID PLAN WAS DEVELOPING, WITH STRAIGHT STREETS CROSSING EACH OTHER AT RIGHT-ANGLES

New York today
Today the city is home to more than 7 million people. It has three main airports and a vast subway with 469 stations. Manhattan is dominated by tall buildings. Some of the large steel-and-glass skyscrapers, such as the Seagram Building, are famous examples of modern architecture. Others, like the World Trade Center, are known for their sheer size. They make ideal headquarters for international companies, and New York is now a world financial and business centre. It is also a cultural centre, with world-famous theatres and galleries serving the vast multi-ethnic population.

ARRIVING SHIPS COULD MOOR AT ONE OF THE MANY WHARVES

A WINDMILL, MOUNTED ON A WOODEN POST, COULD BE TURNED SO THAT THE SAILS FACED THE WIND

New York, 1664
New York City began as a Dutch settlement, called New Amsterdam, on the southern tip of the island of Manhattan. The land had previously belonged to the Carnesie Native Americans. The Dutch settlers built houses with stepped gables, like those in Holland. There was also a windmill, a small harbour, and a fort. Much of the town's wealth came from selling animal skins (otter, mink, and beaver). Tobacco was also grown and traded. In 1664, the English took over the town, naming it New York.

Eco-houses

ARCHITECTS are becoming aware of ways of building that can help the environment – both by reducing their use of scarce resources and by creating eco-houses, homes that are healthier and more pleasant to live in. They begin with the materials, using timber from forests that will be replanted and other materials that can be made without consuming too much energy. As much heat as possible is generated by solar power, and glazed sunspaces allow sunshine to flood the building with warmth and light. Windows need several layers of glass so that this valuable heat is not lost, and lofts need to be insulated so that heat cannot escape through the roof. Facilities for recycling waste and storing water are also important. Even heat can be stored, in rocks hidden beneath the house or a rock-filled core in the middle of the building.

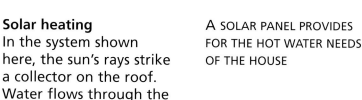

Solar heating

In the system shown here, the sun's rays strike a collector on the roof. Water flows through the collector and is heated. The hot water passes through pipes to a tank where it circulates, heating the water stored there, before passing back to the collector

A SOLAR PANEL PROVIDES FOR THE HOT WATER NEEDS OF THE HOUSE

WATER FLOWS THROUGH PIPES IN THE COLLECTOR

THE WALLS ARE MADE OF NON-TOXIC MATERIALS THAT BLEND INTO THE LOCAL ENVIRONMENT

AN OPENING ROOF LIGHT ALLOWS AIR TO ESCAPE OUT OF THE SUN SPACE

RAINWATER RUNS FROM THE ROOFS AND GUTTERS INTO AN OUTDOOR STORAGE TANK

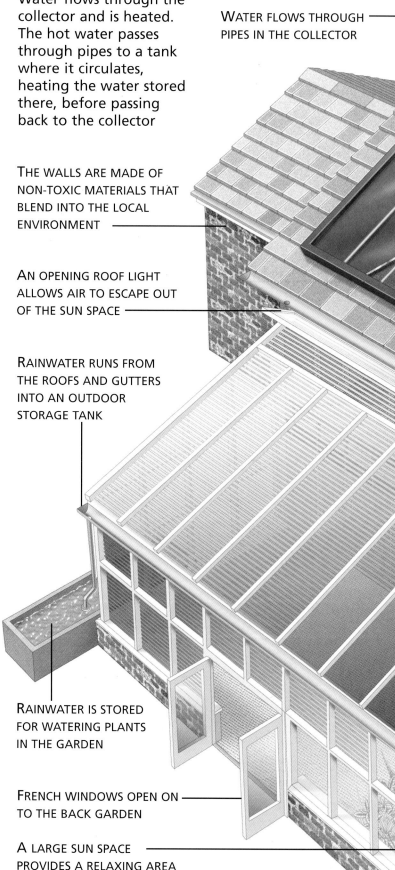

RAINWATER IS STORED FOR WATERING PLANTS IN THE GARDEN

FRENCH WINDOWS OPEN ON TO THE BACK GARDEN

A LARGE SUN SPACE PROVIDES A RELAXING AREA FOR THE SUMMER MONTHS

THIS FRAMEWORK IS BUILT OF TIMBER FROM RENEWABLE FORESTS

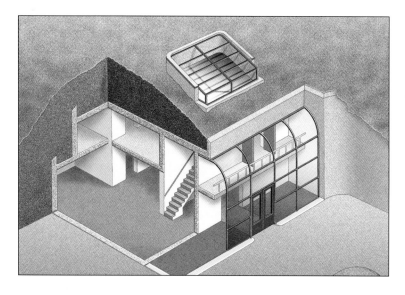

Underground house

A few architects are experimenting with 'earth-sheltered', or underground, houses which fit well into the environment. There can also be heat-saving advantages. The soil around the house heats up very slowly in the summer, so that by the winter, it acts as a warm 'coat' around the house. The soil loses this built-up heat equally slowly, so that it cools the house down in the summer.

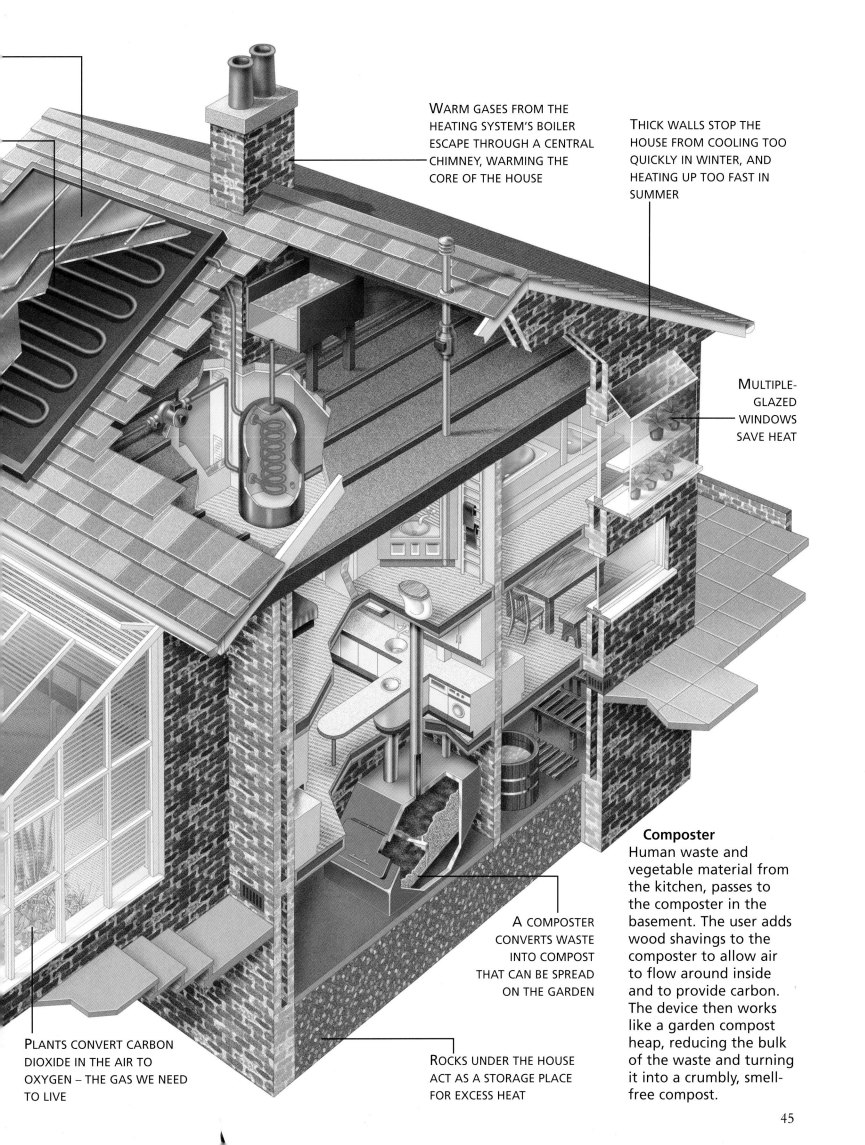

WARM GASES FROM THE HEATING SYSTEM'S BOILER ESCAPE THROUGH A CENTRAL CHIMNEY, WARMING THE CORE OF THE HOUSE

THICK WALLS STOP THE HOUSE FROM COOLING TOO QUICKLY IN WINTER, AND HEATING UP TOO FAST IN SUMMER

MULTIPLE-GLAZED WINDOWS SAVE HEAT

Composter
Human waste and vegetable material from the kitchen, passes to the composter in the basement. The user adds wood shavings to the composter to allow air to flow around inside and to provide carbon. The device then works like a garden compost heap, reducing the bulk of the waste and turning it into a crumbly, smell-free compost.

A COMPOSTER CONVERTS WASTE INTO COMPOST THAT CAN BE SPREAD ON THE GARDEN

PLANTS CONVERT CARBON DIOXIDE IN THE AIR TO OXYGEN – THE GAS WE NEED TO LIVE

ROCKS UNDER THE HOUSE ACT AS A STORAGE PLACE FOR EXCESS HEAT

Index